POETRY OF THE 'NINETIES

Kelsey Thornton, the youngest of three brothers, was born in Huddersfield and brought up over the border in Burnley in an environment of pots, pictures and plays, flavoured with a family enthusiasm for football and motorcycles. He read English at Manchester University, where he won a prize that George Gissing once won, and first became involved with the poets of the 'nineties when he wrote a dissertation on the Rhymers' Club for his Master's degree. After two years as a quite popular but entirely unsuccessful teacher in a grammar school in Devon, he studied for another two years in Manchester before moving in 1965 to take up a post as Lecturer in the Department of English at the University of Newcastle upon Tyne, where he enjoys the post, the place and the people. He is married and has two sons. He buys books, draws, and retains a somewhat abstract passion for motorcycles.

POETRY
OF THE 'NINETIES

EDITED WITH AN INTRODUCTION BY

R. K. R. Thornton

PENGUIN BOOKS

Penguin Books Ltd, Harmondsworth, Middlesex, England
Penguin Books Inc., 7110 Ambassador Road, Baltimore, Maryland 21207, U.S.A.
Penguin Books Australia Ltd, Ringwood, Victoria, Australia

—

First published 1970

—

Copyright © R. K. R. Thornton, 1970

—

Made and printed in Great Britain by
C. Nicholls & Company Ltd
Set in Monotype Perpetua

To the memory of
Peter Ure

CONTENTS

Contents

3. London Types

4. The Hound of Heaven

Contents

5. Love and Death

6. Fire from France

Contents

7. Poems and Ballads

8. The Roses Fall

Contents

ACKNOWLEDGEMENTS

For permission to publish poems in copyright, thanks are due to the following:

for LAURENCE BINYON: to Mrs Nicolette Gray and the Society of Authors, on behalf of the Laurence Binyon Estate;

for OLIVE CUSTANCE: 'The White Statue' from *Opals*, to The Bodley Head;

for LORD ALFRED DOUGLAS: to Mr Edward Colman, on behalf of the Lord Alfred Douglas Literary Estate;

for JOHN GRAY: to the Very Reverend Prior Provincial, O.P., of St Dominic's Priory;

for G. A. GREENE: 'Prelude' from *Italian Lyrists of To-day*, to George Allen & Unwin Ltd;

for THOMAS HARDY: from *The Collected Poems of Thomas Hardy*, reprinted by permission of the Trustees of the Hardy Estate, Macmillan & Co Ltd, London, the Macmillan Company of Canada Ltd and the Macmillan Company Inc., New York. Copyright © 1925 by the Macmillan Company;

for A. E. HOUSMAN: from 'A Shropshire Lad' – authorized edition – from *The Collected Poems of A. E. Housman*. Copyright 1939, 1940, © 1959 by Holt, Rinehart and Winston, Inc. Copyright © 1967, 1968 by Robert E Symons. Reprinted by permission of Holt, Rinehart and Winston, Inc., and the Society of Authors as the literary representative of the Estate of A. E. Housman, and Jonathan Cape Ltd, publishers of A. E. Housman's *Collected Poems*;

for SELWYN IMAGE: from *Poems and Carols*, to George Allen & Unwin Ltd;

for RUDYARD KIPLING: from *Barrack-Room Ballads* and *Rudyard Kipling's Verse: Definitive Edition*, to Mrs George Bambridge, Methuen & Co Ltd, Macmillan & Co Ltd and Doubleday & Company, Inc.;

for RICHARD LE GALLIENNE: to the Society of Authors as the literary representative of The Estate of Richard Le Gallienne;

Acknowledgements

for ALICE MEYNELL: to Mrs S. Mulvey and the Meynell Family Properties Ltd;

for HENRY NEWBOLT: from *Poems: New and Old*, published by John Murray, to Mr Peter Newbolt;

for VINCENT O'SULLIVAN: from *Poems*, to George Allen & Unwin Ltd;

for VICTOR PLARR: from *In the Dorian Mood*, to The Bodley Head;

for ARTHUR SYMONS: from *The Poems of Arthur Symons*, to William Heinemann Ltd and Dodd, Mead & Company Inc.;

for THEODORE WRATISLAW: to Richards Press Ltd;

for W. B. YEATS: from *Collected Poems of W. B. Yeats*, published by Macmillan, to Mr M. B. Yeats and Macmillan & Co Ltd, London.

Every effort has been made to trace copyright holders, but in a few cases this has proved impossible. The publishers would be interested to hear from any copyright holders not here acknowledged.

Note

I should like to thank the University of Newcastle upon Tyne for, among other less tangible things, an award from the University Research Fund which enabled me to visit the British Museum to consult some of the more obscure volumes. I also wish to thank the staff of the British Museum for their help, and the staff of Newcastle libraries, the University library, the City Library and the library of the Literary and Philosophical Society, who made it easier to carry out most of the work in Newcastle.

R. K. R. THORNTON

INTRODUCTION

It is common to look at the 1890s as a coherent period; before the nineteenth century had ended, Max Beerbohm had looked back to 'the Beardsley period', and the sense of the decade's form epitomizes its own self-consciousness and self-dramatization. This form has been described. in important books about the period: Holbrook Jackson's *The Eighteen Nineties* (1913), Richard Le Gallienne's *The Romantic '90s* (1926), and in particular W. B. Yeats's impressive piece of mythologizing, the *Autobiographies* (1926), of which 'The Tragic Generation' (1922) forms a part; and the form has been illustrated by anthologies, notably those excellent compilations made by A. J. A. Symons (1928) and Martin Secker (1948). Although each book added its own detail, its own angle, there was a large ground of general agreement and the present selection does not try to get rid of the 'nineties myth. It does, however, recognize that the myth can be limiting and includes poems which qualify it. The poems, which are after all the chief point and interest of an anthology, were chosen to illustrate not a thesis but a period; but they encouraged a close look at some common generalizations about 'nineties writers and their work. This introduction looks at these generalizations and suggests reasons why we might qualify our acceptance of them.

The most common picture of the 'nineties, always good copy and encouraged of late by the boom in Beardsley, is of the sensational type, sees the period as 'Decadent' and usually takes as its central symbol *The Yellow Book*, the publication of which marked a significant step in the crystallization of 'nineties myths. The first volume, in April 1894, was greeted with howls of protest. The *Westminster Gazette* went so far as to say of two of Beardsley's drawings in it that nothing they knew 'would meet the case except a short Act of Parliament to make this kind of thing illegal'. *The Times* said that 'it might be intended to attract by its very repulsiveness and insolence, and in that case it is not unlikely to be successful'. Even in private the reaction was the same: two maiden ladies who wrote poems and passionate dramas under the name of 'Michael Field' and were by no means reactionary, had an interest in the publication, since they had sent a poem for inclusion in the second volume. They wrote in their diary:

We have been almost blinded by the glare of hell.... As we came up to the shop we found the whole frontage a hot background of orange-colour to sly, roistering heads, silhouetted against it and half-hiding behind masks. The window seemed to be gibbering, our eyes to be filled with incurable jaundice. *La Réclame*, hideous beyond Duessa or any Witch ever seen by the mind's eyes, stood up before us as a shop where contemporary literature is sold. One felt as one does when now and then a wholly lost woman stands flaming on the pavement with the ghastly laugh of the ribald crowd in the air round her. One hates one's eyes for seeing! But the infamous window mocked and mowed and fizgiged, saffron and pitchy, till one's eyes were arrested like Virgil's before the wind of flame.

And the inside of the book! It is full of cleverness such as one expects to find in those who dwell below light and hope and love and aspiration.[1]

Little wonder then that they demanded the return of their poem.

The Yellow Book was, in short, a red rag to John Bull. Those who had produced its daring image (deliberately taking the colour of the yellow-backed French novels) did their work

1. B.M. Add. MS. 46782, p. 70.

only too well. Writers, artists and publishers had learned, usually from France, that there was much to be gained from outrageous attitudes: the artist could have his fun at the expense of the bourgeois, on whom he nonetheless depended, by laughing at the shocked response which greeted each new venture; he could feel comfortably superior because of his more sophisticated and tolerant attitudes; and at the same time he could further the serious cause of his art. Knowing the power of advertisement (had not Oscar Wilde been made famous beyond his talent through parody and shocked fascination?), satirists and players of the game of *épater le bourgeois* throve on each other, and from the popularity of some of the productions, even the bourgeois enjoyed the game. But in the case of *The Yellow Book*, the exercise in shocking the bourgeois was too successful, especially when the sense of outrage at the immorality of art was strengthened by such equally well-publicized scandals as the case of Oscar Wilde (the yellow-backed French novel he carried at the time of his arrest was reported in the papers as 'Yellow Book'). Because of its success, the one outraged response is often all that is remembered, and the variety of the period is obscured by the assumption that the 'nineties can be summed up in one of those favourite adjectives, 'naughty' or 'decadent'.

To balance the caricature Decadent, one finds at the other extreme the Anti-decadent or activist, the muscular moral imperialist. The case is nicely summed up by the first words of Professor J. H. Buckley's preface to his *William Ernest Henley: A Study in the 'Counter-Decadence' of the 'Nineties*:

By some tacit agreement literary historians of the Victorian period have isolated a picturesque movement dominated by the hero-villain Oscar Wilde and known as the 'decadence' of the 'yellow 'nineties.' The convenience of such a label has led many a reader virtually to ignore the truly vital writing of the English *fin de siècle*. For if there was in the 'nineties a 'decadent' coterie, there was also a far more vigorous 'counter-decadent' group.

This group gathered round the *National Observer* under the editorship of W. E. Henley, and was dubbed by Beerbohm the 'Henley Regatta'. The most obvious example of the type of poetical vigour which this man of passion inspired or attracted to him is Kipling, though Yeats was also among those whose work he published (incidentally revising without Yeats's permission).

Both these caricatures are to be found in the satires of the period itself, although the Decadent was by far the more popular, both because he was simpler to caricature, and because laughter and the desire to mock are more often the province of the vigorous element. Owen Seaman, in *The Battle of the Bays* (1894), which brilliantly parodies poets who might have been considered for the Laureateship on the death of Tennyson, wrote in 'A Ballad of a Bun' of a would-be-popular lady writer seeking the way to success:

> A Decadent was dribbling by;
>   'Lady,' he said, 'you seem undone;
> You need a panacea; try
>   This sample of the Bodley bun.
>
> 'It is fulfilled of precious spice,
>   Whereof I give the recipe; –
> Take common dripping, stew in vice,
>   And serve with vertu; taste and see!
>
> 'And lo! I brand you on the brow
>   As kin to Nature's lowest germ;
> You are sister to the microbe now,
>   And second-cousin to the worm.'

This parody of Davidson's 'A Ballad of a Nun' (see p. 195) already contains the ingredients of the picture of the Decadent that became so popular. It even includes a reference to the Bodley Head, under which sign John Lane and Elkin Mathews published. Together they began *The Yellow Book*, though Mathews left Lane after the second volume, and they published many of the interesting writers of the decade; their list of 1894 includes Laurence Binyon, John Davidson, 'Michael Field', Herbert Horne, Lionel Johnson, Richard Le Gallienne, Alice Meynell, Dollie Radford, Francis Thompson, Ernest Rhys, and Oscar Wilde, not to mention the *Book of the Rhymers' Club* with its contributions by Dowson, Symons and Yeats. Because of the limitations of Lane's list, Seaman called him

> a sorry sort of Lane
> That hardly ever turns aside,

but he was able to see the value of controversy and published Seaman himself; and he was sufficiently turned aside by the scandal to withdraw Wilde's works from the list. The only other publisher of comparable importance was Leonard Smithers, whose combination of pornography with the best in recent art and literature indicates the place to which public opinion had thrust art in the shocked reaction of the later 1890s. It was Smithers who published *The Savoy* (1896) when *The Yellow Book*, dismissing Beardsley because rumour wrongly associated him with Wilde, lost most of its crusading zeal. *The Savoy*, edited by Arthur Symons and Aubrey Beardsley, was the only English magazine which can justly be called Symbolist, yet in its day it too was lumped with the rest, as in this comment by Ernest Rhys in *The Literary Year-Book* of 1897:

As for the 'Decadence', some of the younger men who have been most freely displaying its colours during the year, as in the derelict 'Savoy', Mr Symons and (I fear) Mr Yeats, are gone south, only to return, let us hope, under a crescent star! The century's end, then, need not prove quite fatal.

The place of the 'nineties in literary history, where it is sometimes regarded as a dead end, is somewhat clarified if one sees the close relationship of Decadence to Symbolism, which had a much wider influence. Symons's *The Symbolist Movement in Literature* (1899), which led Eliot to discover Laforgue and the other French Symbolists, is a later form of a book announced earlier as *The Decadent Movement in Literature*. In the Introduction Symons described how 'the interlude, half a mock-interlude, of Decadence, diverted the attention of the critics while something more serious was in preparation', namely Symbolism.

The Decadent, however, was much more simple to satirize than the Symbolist, and Seaman was not the only one to take advantage of the fact. *Punch* even ran a series of cartoons about 'Our Decadents', and no comic paper could be without its shaft at the popular butt. The character of the Decadent had been established in France in 1884 when J. K. Huysmans wrote *À Rebours*, a novel whose hero, des Esseintes, the last in an aristocratic line, attempts to live a life where, cut off from the outside world and surrounded by art and the artificial, he rather than nature will control his existence. Among the most complete satirical pictures of the Decadent in the 'nineties is that by Lionel Johnson, classical scholar, poet, and critic of some wit and perception. His essay, 'The Cultured Faun', published in the *Anti-Jacobin* in 1891, summarizes the characteristics of the beast:

Externally, our hero should cultivate a reassuring sobriety of habit, with just a dash of the dandy. None of the wandering looks, the elaborate disorder, the sublime lunacy of his predecessor, the 'apostle of culture'. Externally, then, a precise appearance;

internally, a catholic sympathy with all that exists, and 'therefore' suffers, for art's sake. Now art, at present, is not a question of the senses so much as of the nerves. Botticelli, indeed, was very precious, but Baudelaire is very nervous. Gautier was adorably sensuous, but M. Verlaine is pathetically sensitive. That is the point: exquisite appreciation of pain, exquisite thrills of anguish, exquisite adoration of suffering. Here comes in a tender patronage of Catholicism: white tapers upon the high altar, an ascetic and beautiful young priest, the great gilt monstrance, the subtle-scented and mystical incense, the old world accents of the Vulgate, of the Holy Offices; the splendour of the sacred vestments. We kneel at some hour, not too early for our convenience, repeating the solemn Latin, drinking in those Gregorian tones, with plenty of modern French sonnets in memory, should the sermon be dull. But to join the Church! Ah, no! better to dally with the enchanting mysteries, to pass from our dreams of delirium to our dreams of sanctity with no coarse facts to jar upon us. And so these refined persons cherish a double 'passion', the sentiment of repentant yearning and the sentiment of rebellious sin.

To play the part properly a flavour of cynicism is recom-mended: a scientific profession of materialist dogmas, coupled – for you should forswear consistency – with gloomy chatter about 'The Will to Live'.... Jumble all these 'impressions' together, your sympathies and your sorrows, your devotion and your des-pair; carry them about with you in a state of fermentation, and finally conclude that life is loathsome yet that beauty is beatific. And beauty – ah, beauty is everything beautiful! Isn't that a trifle obvious, you say? That is the charm of it, it shows your perfect simplicity, your chaste and catholic innocence. Innocence of course: beauty is always innocent, ultimately. No doubt there are 'monstrous' things, terrible pains, the haggard eyes of an *absin-theur*, the pallid faces of 'neurotic' sinners; but all that is the portion of our Parisian friends, such and such a 'group of artists', who meet at the Café So-and-So. We like people to think we are much the same, but it isn't true. We are quite harmless, we only concoct strange and subtle verse about it. And, anyway, beauty includes everything; there's another sweet saying for you from our 'impressionist' copy-books. Impressions! that is all. Life is mean and vulgar, Members of Parliament are odious, the critics are commercial pedants: we alone know Beauty, and Art, and Sorrow and Sin. Impressions! exquisite, dainty fantasies; fiery-coloured visions; and impertinence straggling into epigram, for 'the true' criticism; *c'est adorable!* And since we are scholars and none of your penny-a-line Bohemians, we throw in occasional doses of 'Hellenism': by which we mean the Ideal of the Cultured Faun. That is to say, a flowery Paganism, such as no 'Pagan' ever had; a mixture of 'beautiful woodland natures', and 'the perfect come-liness of the Parthenon frieze', together with the elegant languors and favourite vices of (let us parade our 'decadent' learning) the *Stratonis Epigrammata*. At this time of day we need not dilate upon the equivocal charm of everything Lesbian. And who shall assail us? – what stupid and uncultured critic, what coarse and narrow Philistine? We are the Elect of Beauty: saints and sinners, devils and devotees, Athenians and Parisians, Romans of the Empire and Italians of the Renaissance. *Fin de siècle! Fin de siècle!* Literature is a thing of beauty, blood, and nerves.

Though it is quite clear that Johnson, like his 'Philistine critic', thinks this creature a 'feeble and foolish beast', he himself is sometimes represented as a similar sort of character.

It is essential to be clear, then, that the Decadent and the Anti-decadent are caricatures, or at best pictures which are only occasionally true to the life. Johnson obviously saw the pitfalls too clearly to be himself a Decadent. Yeats, a con-tributor to the *National Observer*, and even referred to by Henley as 'one of my lads',[2] is often, and with accuracy, associated with the so-called Decadent groups. Richard Le Gallienne, though he tried to dissociate himself from them by writing *English Poems* (1892), *The Religion of a Literary Man* (1893), and satires like 'The Décadent to his Soul', wrote poems which make it simple to include him among

2. W. B. Yeats, *Autobiographies*, 1955, p. 129.

Decadent writers. Most poets of the 'nineties have at one time or another been called Decadent, though critics who examine their work in greater detail usually remark on the inaccuracy of the term. Even the biographer of Arthur Symons, the writer most closely associated with the movement, insists that 'it would be fallacious to confine him, as has already been done, solely within those narrow limits'.[3] *The Yellow Book* is misleadingly caricatured; Sir Frederick Leighton, P.R.A., Henry James, William Watson, and W. B. Yeats, all of whom contributed to the first volume, do not seem 'below light and hope', and time has faded even the most outrageous of the other contributions. Amidst its reputedly hothouse climate grew some very ordinary blooms, just as in the books of the Rhymers' Club, whose atmosphere was recently described by an American Professor as 'hectic and overstrained', one can find a poem like T. W. Rolleston's 'Cycling Song', whose fate as a school song accurately suggests the degree of its exoticism. Yet, though it is a critical commonplace to insist on qualifications of the picture, the simplifications persist; myths and patterns are more powerful than objective truth, and we are unlikely to lose the division between what Lionel Johnson called the pallid school and the school of fresh and vigorous blood.

This is not necessarily a bad thing. The simplifications have their uses; it is convenient to have one's literary history made into a simple pattern, partaking, as Dr Johnson wrote, 'of the spirit of history, which is contrary to minute exactness'. The pattern can often convey the flavour of an age more forcibly than mere pedantic insistence on fact. After all, the myths are influenced, usually created, by men who lived through the period; it is often their lives and their work that we wish to understand, and

3. Roger Lhombreaud, *Arthur Symons: A Critical Biography*, 1963, p. 61.

the meaning of the events is contained in their shaping of them. Thus we have Yeats's description of his friends as 'The Tragic Generation'. Writers about the period support the idea of tragedy with a list of those who died young: Dowson at thirty-two, Johnson at thirty-five, Beardsley at twenty-five, Crackanthorpe at twenty-seven, Wilde at forty-six; one even finds Davidson, a suicide in 1909 at the age of fifty-three, among the young deaths of the 'nineties. It is useless to point to the reasonable survival rate of the Rhymers' Club for example (only three out of thirteen failed to reach the age of sixty); or to compare the loss of poetic talent to the early 1820s when Keats died at twenty-five, Shelley at twenty-nine, and Byron at thirty-six. Tragedies are not comparative, and while the latter deaths seem like accidental cutting off of talent, the deaths of the writers of the 'nineties seem a sort of fulfilment. Yeats conveyed the sense of decline and tragedy which those deaths symbolize, and the final section of this anthology shows how common the sense of tragedy was, and how it marks the poems as well as the lives of the poets.

Symons too created myths out of the raw material of his friends' lives, most obviously in his account of Dowson, who is often taken as a representative Decadent and typical 'nineties poet. The process of Dowson's mythification is instructive, showing the struggle between the truth to fact and the truth to the spirit. Symons's 'A literary Causerie: on a Book of Verses', in *The Savoy* of August 1896, was a picture of Dowson though it did not mention his name. Treating Dowson almost as if he were already dead, Symons depicted a *poète maudit*, a man of dilapidated appearance, a lover of the sordid in his surroundings, an experimenter with drugs ('At Oxford, I believe, his favourite form of intoxication had been haschisch,' wrote Symons), and a seeker of oblivion, usually through drink. This image of

Dowson, reiterated by Symons in his obituary notice of the poet, and in the introduction to an edition of Dowson's poems, was strengthened by Yeats's stories and impressions in his *Autobiographies*, and has usually done service as a version of Dowson for the literary histories ever since, influencing also the interpretation of his poems. Friends who knew him better than Symons did and scholars who have studied his life and work have repeatedly tried to rectify the errors in the picture (Edgar Jepson in 1907 and again in 1933, Victor Plarr in 1914, Desmond Flower in 1934, 1950 and 1967, John Gawsworth in 1938, Mark Longaker in 1944 and 1968, and Russell Goldfarb in 1964). The myth persists, attracting readers to his poems, but making misreadings of them too common. Most ironic of all, a letter from Dowson to Symons which has recently come to light suggests that, though Dowson reacted against the description 'dilapidated', he did not object as strongly to the picture as his defenders have. Feeling himself 'fortunate in my chronicler',[4] he was willing to be part of a myth.

Elements of 'nineties history and criticism are usefully summarized by using the two caricatured extremes. The trial of Oscar Wilde, for example, can be seen as a debate between Decadent and Anti-decadent literary theory. Wilde had been made to defend at his first trial his aphorism that there was no such thing as a moral or an immoral book, and he contended that a book was either well or badly written. When the Marquess of Queensberry's accusations against Wilde were apparently proved, the Anti-decadent faction of the *National Observer* was among the most vociferous in its denunciation of Wilde and the theory of art he stood for:

There is not a man or woman in the English-speaking world possessed of the treasure of a wholesome mind who is not under a

4. Desmond Flower and Henry Maas, eds., *The Letters of Ernest Dowson*, 1967, p. 371.

deep debt of gratitude to the Marquess of Queensberry for destroying the High Priest of the Decadents. The obscene impostor, whose prominence has been a social outrage ever since he transferred from Trinity Dublin to Oxford his vices, his follies, and his vanities, has been exposed, and that thoroughly at last. But to the exposure there must be legal and social sequels. There must be another trial at the Old Bailey, or a coroner's inquest – the latter for choice; and of the Decadents, of their hideous conceptions of the meaning of Art, of their worse than Eleusinian mysteries, there must be an absolute end.[5]

These two views explain somewhat the sensation the trial caused in literary circles. Despite the blasts of morality which followed, Arthur Symons stuck to his artistic principles and summarized the position in the preface to the second edition of his *Silhouettes* (1896):

... a work of art can be judged from only two standpoints: the standpoint from which its art is measured entirely by its morality, and the standpoint from which its morality is measured entirely by its art.

Symons saw the same sort of division in the use of the word 'Decadence', 'either hurled as a reproach or hurled back as a defiance'. Again the caricature extremes provide a useful way of understanding the term: on the one hand a term of abuse for the Anti-decadent critic, who was hostile, aggressively masculine, anti-French, pro-British, and above all concerned with content and its morality; on the other hand a descriptive term for the Decadent writer, who applied it to style, with which he was most concerned, believing in the irrelevance of morality in artistic matters, inclined to a feminine sensitivity, French-loving. Between the two extremes come the infinite gradations, but the caricatures serve to heighten the distinctions.

One does not always wish to distinguish; if there is a

5. Quoted in *Famous Trials 7: Oscar Wilde*, 1962.

division on the point of morality, there is yet agreement in some respects on the craft of poetry, agreement which can be related to the work of Walter Pater. Pater was perhaps not the man whom one would have expected to inspire seekers after beauty. Beerbohm was so disappointed in Pater's appearance at Oxford that he reported in 'Dimi-nuendo' that 'I nearly went down when they told me that this was Pater'. But, speaking of the new generation of writers in the 'nineties, Yeats remarked in *The Oxford Book of Modern Verse* that 'one writer . . . had its entire uncritical admiration', and that was Pater. From him came not only a love of learning and a philosophy that helped cause the dis-asters, but also three important features of the 'nineties aesthetic: the demand for freedom of choice in subject matter, the impressionistic style, and the notion of the musicality of verse.

The search for new subject matter was not understood alike by master and disciples. Pater took away the 'Con-clusion' to his *Studies in the History of the Renaissance*, fearing that his work 'might possibly mislead some of those young men into whose hands it might fall'. Yeats recorded in his *Autobiographies* how Lionel Johnson, whose word was not always to be trusted, came back from a visit to Pater with the story that, having commented on some books on economics on Pater's shelves, he had been assured by Pater that 'nothing that has interested mankind can ever lose that interest'. However accurate the report, Johnson's story was true to the ideas that Pater put into his criticism. Writers derived a demand for freedom of subject matter and a notion of the amorality of art from such comments in the 'Conclusion' as 'not the fruit of experience, but experience itself, is the end'; or 'art comes to you profess-ing frankly to give nothing but the highest quality to your moments as they pass, and simply for those moments' sake'.

Yeats, in the *Autobiographies*, argued along Paterian lines that:

Science, through much ridicule and some persecution has won the right to explore whatever passes before its corporeal eye, and merely because it passes.... Literature now demands the same right of exploration of all that passes before the mind's eye, and merely because it passes.

Richard Le Gallienne, in *The Romantic '90s*, described Davidson's 'note of revolt against conventional hypocrisies, and his vindication of the free play of human vitality'. Symons too is Paterian at the end of the Introduction to the second edition of *London Nights* (1897), where he claimed that 'whatever has existed has achieved the right of artistic existence'. The question is summed up by Symons in *Silhouettes* (1896) where he wrote, 'If we are to save people's souls by the writing of verses, well and good. But if not, there is no choice but to admit absolute freedom of choice.'

Henley with his hospital poems, Kipling with his ballads of common soldiers, and both in their introduction of a hitherto 'unpoetic' vocabulary, the idiom of the street or the barrack-room, were making advances in new material for poetry, as was Davidson, whose work Eliot saw as an element in his own development. (See the Introduction to section 3 of this anthology.)

Novelty was sought in both the 'physical life' and the 'inward world of thought and feeling', to use Pater's division. In this era of the early psychoanalysts, both artists and writers were fond of the image of the reflection, and examined the complexities of their own moods and ideas, and that 'unseen reality apprehended by the consciousness', which is what Symons said Symbolism attempts to express. One is reminded of Hopkins's novel vocabulary, and his search for the inner nature of an object through exact realization of it.

Catching the exact nature of the thing described is the second feature of 'nineties writing that may be owed to Pater, and this more closely unites the two camps. Arnold had written in *On Translating Homer* (1861) that 'of the literature of France and Germany, as of the intellect in Europe in general, the main effort, for now many years, has been a critical effort; the endeavour in all branches of knowledge, theology, philosophy, history, art, science, to see the object as in itself it really is'. Pater, in *The Renaissance*, acknowledged the justice of Arnold's statement, but added that 'in aesthetic criticism the first step towards seeing one's object as it really is, is to know one's own impression as it really is, to discriminate it, to realize it distinctly'. The method of realizing the impression and fixing it is suggested by another comment of Pater that 'the first condition of the poetic way of seeing and presenting things is particularization'. One thus finds theory and practice concerned with the impression. Ernest Dowson wrote in the novel on which he and Arthur Moore collaborated, *Adrian Rome* (1899):

The fulness of one's life, the fineness of one's impressions, the multiplicity of one's sensations; here it seemed to him, was the rough material out of which grew magnificently the ultimate achievement of one's art.

Symons claimed that Verlaine had achieved the ideal of Decadence, which was 'to fix the last fine shade, the quintessence of things; to fix it fleetingly'.[6] And in the same essay he says of Henley that 'the poetry of Impressionism can go no further, in one direction, than that series of rhymes and rhythms named *In Hospital*'. This is not mere perversity on Symons's part, for Shaw too saw that Henley's

6. Arthur Symons, 'The Decadent Movement in Literature', *Harper's*, 1893.

chief quality lay in his ability to 'describe anything that was forced on his observation and experience, from a tom-cat in an area to a hospital operation'.[7]

The practice of this style, and its influence, can most simply be seen by looking at a few lines of Symons, and comparing them with some of Eliot. From Symons's 'White Heliotrope':

> The feverish room and that white bed,
> The tumbled skirts upon a chair,
> The novel flung half-open, where
> Hat, hair-pins, puffs, and paints, are spread.

The pictorial arrangement, the eighteenth-century ability to let juxtaposition do the commenting, the impersonality, these are common in Eliot's poems too:

> Out of the window perilously spread
> Her drying combinations touched by the sun's last rays,
> On the divan are piled (at night her bed)
> Stockings, slippers, camisoles, and stays.

Equally important is the idea of the musicality of verse, another feature of 'nineties poetry which finds its way into Eliot's poems, as in the *Four Quartets* or 'Rhapsody on a Windy Night'. The idea is expressed most famously in Pater's remark in 'The School of Giorgione' that 'all art constantly aspires towards the condition of music'. What he meant was that the arts all attempt to achieve an inseparability of form and content such as one finds in music, an idea developed in the image of the dancer, whose rhythmic movement cannot be separated from her, and who symbolizes a complex set of associated ideas in the poems and paintings of the period. But music, Pater had said, 'is the true measure of perfected art', and, though he may not

7. Letter to Archibald Henderson, in Henderson's *George Bernard Shaw: His Life and Works*, 1911.

have followed writers like Baudelaire, who described in his 'Correspondances' how 'perfumes, colours and sounds answer each other', his ideas were echoed by French and English writers. Where Verlaine demanded 'music before all else', Dowson wrote to Arthur Moore that he was writing 'verses making for mere sound, & music, with just a suggestion of sense, or hardly that'.[8] Yeats spoke of Dowson's poems as 'not speech but perfect song, though song for the speaking voice'.

To use the vocabulary of one art for another was common: Beardsley in a letter quoted by his recent biographer wrote of 'story painters and picture writers',[9] John Gray wrote *Silverpoints*, Whistler painted 'Harmonies', Wilde wrote a 'Symphony in Yellow', Henley composed 'London Voluntaries'. Arthur Symons even saw 'The World as Ballet', and artists strove to achieve a unified composition in their lives as well as their art.

Though there are important distinctions between groups of writers, there is a certain amount of common ground provided by the three features that I have mentioned. These also suggest something of the debt to the 'nineties that was felt by later poets. Pound, for example, whose poem 'The Decadence' is (I hope) a parody which indicates a thorough understanding of the subject, wrote the 'Imagist Triad'as a statement of the aims of Imagism:

1. Direct treatment of the 'thing' whether subjective or objective.
2. To use absolutely no word that does not contribute to the presentation.
3. As regarding rhythm: to compose in the sequence of the musical phrase, not in sequence of a metronome.[10]

8. Desmond Flower and Henry Maas, eds., *The Letters of Ernest Dowson*, 1967, p. 190
9. Stanley Weintraub, *Beardsley*, 1967, p. 95.
10. *Make It New*, 1934.

Other poets learned from or with the 'nineties poets, but there is no need to justify the latter by suggesting their place in the background of modern literature; they are themselves sufficiently attractive and varied to demand the attention of a new anthology.

All this qualification of accepted pictures might lead the reader to think that I intend to put forward now an anthology providing a 'true likeness'; but one can do no more than provide another version. I have selected poems published between 1890 and 1900 which reflect both the quality and the interest of work in the period. A few of Henley's poems belong to some years earlier, but were substantially revised and largely made their mark in the 'nineties, a few were written in the period but not published, such as Dowson's 'Against My Lady Burton', and one, Hardy's 'The Darkling Thrush', belongs in this company by virtue of its moment of conception. I have selected only complete poems, feeling that to select extracts would not reflect the concern with form which marks the period. Some of the poems are, however, detached from a series. The poems are divided into eight more or less coherent groups which arise from the poems rather than from an imposed plan, and their arrangement within the sections is designed to provide comparisons and contrasts which may be informative; to place, for example, Yeats among those

> Poets with whom I learned my trade,
> Companions of the Cheshire Cheese.[11]

The 'true likeness' is an impossible ideal, and to come near it would require space for poems, plays, short stories, pictures, drawings, photographs, music, song, dance. This selection is merely intended to capture something of the

11. 'The Grey Rock.'

attractiveness of 'nineties poetry and convey its pleasures without pinning it out for demonstration like a bright, slightly dusty but completely dead butterfly.

R. K. R. THORNTON

A NOTE ON THE TEXT

Each poem is followed by the author's name and the name and date of the volume from which the text is taken. This date does not always accurately reflect the date of composition, and details of writing and publishing history must be sought in the books listed in the bibliography. I have omitted some dates given by the poets themselves, to avoid confusion and because they are not always accurate. I have also omitted the dedications which some of the poets placed before their poems, because, although this 'nineties fad would give something of a period flavour, the dedications are irrelevant to the poems.

R. K. R. T.

1. *All the Arts*

ALL THE ARTS

'THE first duty in life is to be as artificial as possible. What the second duty is no one has as yet discovered.' In this typically self-conscious epigram from his 'Phrases and Philosophies for the Use of the Young', Wilde summed up the late nineteenth-century artist's contention that Art is superior to Nature. The same notion was symbolized by his notorious green carnation; flowers were more acceptable if they were artificially aided. Max Beerbohm, flippantly penetrating to the essence of the subject in his 'A Defence of Cosmetics', wrote that 'we are ripe for a new epoch of artifice'. The outraged critics of *The Yellow Book*, where this essay appeared, did not seem to see Beerbohm's satiric purpose, even when he pointed it out in the second volume; for his analysis seemed only too accurate.

Baudelaire, in his 'Éloge du Maquillage', had pointed out the connexion between cosmetics and morals, arguing that, whereas crime is natural, virtue is artificial, so that the application of make-up is a praiseworthy attempt to rise above the natural. 'Evil happens effortlessly, *naturally*, fatally,' wrote Baudelaire; 'good is always the product of some art.' Beerbohm leaned heavily on these ideas when he wrote in the essay mentioned above that

the era of rouge is upon us, and as only in an elaborate era can man by the tangled accrescency of his own pleasures and emotions reach that refinement which is his highest excellence, and by making himself, so to say, independent of Nature, come nearest to God, so only in an elaborate era is woman perfect. Artifice is the strength of the world.

Yeats demonstrated his commitment to the same ideas when he quoted from an early diary of his:

> If we cannot imagine ourselves as different from what we are, and try to assume that second self, we cannot impose a discipline upon ourselves though we may accept one from others. Active virtue, as distinguished from the passive acceptance of a code, is therefore theatrical, consciously dramatic, the wearing of a mask.[1]

Make-up, morality, the mask, theatre, music-hall, dancers and the dance, the remaking of the self, all forms of artifice, thus form an interesting set of interconnected ideas, perhaps clearest in the work of Arthur Symons.

Writers were self-conscious, drawing their images from literature and art as Beardsley did his pictures, and frequently using art or artists as subject matter. 'La Gioconda' for example is one of a book of poems whose starting point is a picture, and incidentally it recalls the passage of Pater which Yeats made the first piece in his *Oxford Book of Modern Verse*. Life itself was also an art. The attitude of the dandy, whether English or French, fact or fiction, whether Baudelaire, Beardsley, Beerbohm, or the des Esseintes of *À Rebours*, was summed up in those words of Wilde that André Gide reported: 'I have put my genius into my life; I have put merely my talent into my work.' Though some were accused of posing, the dandy's concern with creating himself reflects a fundamental part of the aesthetic of the most influential writers of the day, the placing of the artificial above the natural.

1. *Mythologies*, 1962, p. 334.

VILLANELLE OF THE POET'S ROAD

Wine and woman and song,
　Three things garnish our way:
Yet is day over long.

Lest we do our youth wrong,
　Gather them while we may:
Wine and woman and song.

Three things render us strong,
　Vine leaves, kisses and bay;
Yet is day over long.

Unto us they belong,
　Us the bitter and gay,
Wine and woman and song.

We, as we pass along,
　Are sad that they will not stay;
Yet is day over long.

Fruits and flowers among,
　What is better than they:
Wine and woman and song?
　Yet is day over long.

ERNEST DOWSON
Decorations (1899)

ORCHIDS

Orange and purple, shot with white and mauve,
Such in a greenhouse wet with tropic heat
One sees these delicate flowers whose parents throve
In some Pacific island's hot retreat.

Their ardent colours that betray the rank
Fierce hotbed of corruption whence they rose
Please eyes that long for stranger sweets than prank
Wild meadow-blooms and what the garden shows.

Exotic flowers! How great is my delight
To watch your petals curiously wrought,
To lie among your splendours day and night
Lost in a subtle dream of subtler thought.

Bathed in your clamorous orchestra of hues,
The palette of your perfumes, let me sleep
While your mesmeric presences diffuse
Weird dreams: and then bizarre sweet rhymes shall creep

Forth from my brain and slowly form and make
Sweet poems as a weaving spider spins,
A shrine of loves that laugh and swoon and ache,
A temple of coloured sorrows and perfumed sins!

THEODORE WRATISLAW
Orchids (1896)

BAUDELAIRE

A Paris gutter of the good old times,
   Black and putrescent in its stagnant bed,
   Save where the shamble oozings fringe it red,
Or scaffold trickles, or nocturnal crimes.

It holds dropped gold; dead flowers from tropic climes;
   Gems true and false, by midnight maskers shed;
   Old pots of rouge; old broken phials that spread
Vague fumes of musk, with fumes from slums and slimes.

And everywhere, as glows the set of day,
   There floats upon the winding fetid mire
The gorgeous iridescence of decay:

A wavy film of colour, gold and fire,
   Trembles all through it as you pick your way,
And streaks of purple that are straight from Tyre.

EUGENE LEE-HAMILTON
Sonnets of the Wingless Hours (1894)

HOTHOUSE FLOWERS

I hate the flower of wood or common field.
I cannot love the primrose nor regret
The death of any shrinking violet,
Nor even the cultured garden's banal yield.

The silver lips of lilies virginal,
The full deep bosom of the enchanted rose
Please less than flowers glass-hid from frosts and snows
For whom an alien heat makes festival.

I love those flowers reared by man's careful art,
Of heady scents and colours : strong of heart
Or weak that die beneath the touch or knife,

Some rich as sin and some as virtue pale,
And some as subtly infamous and frail
As she whose love still eats my soul and life.

THEODORE WRATISLAW
Orchids (1896)

DÉCOR DE THÉÂTRE

I. BEHIND THE SCENES · EMPIRE

The little painted angels flit,
    See, down the narrow staircase, where
The pink legs flicker over it!

Blonde, and bewigged, and winged with gold,
    The shining creatures of the air
Troop sadly, shivering with cold.

The gusty gaslight shoots a thin
    Sharp finger over cheeks and nose
Rouged to the colour of the rose.

All wigs and paint, they hurry in :
    Then, bid their radiant moment be
The footlights' immortality!

ARTHUR SYMONS
London Nights (2nd edition 1897)

PROLOGUE

My life is like a music-hall,
   Where, in the impotence of rage,
Chained by enchantment to my stall,
   I see myself upon the stage
Dance to amuse a music-hall.

'Tis I that smoke this cigarette,
   Lounge here, and laugh for vacancy,
And watch the dancers turn; and yet
   It is my very self I see
Across the cloudy cigarette.

My very self that turns and trips,
   Painted, pathetically gay,
An empty song upon the lips
   In make-believe of holiday:
I, I, this thing that turns and trips!

The light flares in the music-hall,
   The light, the sound, that weary us;
Hour follows hour, I count them all,
   Lagging, and loud, and riotous:
My life is like a music-hall.

ARTHUR SYMONS
London Nights (2nd edition 1897)

THE MUSIC-HALL

The curtain on the grouping dancers falls,
The heaven of colour has vanished from our eyes;
Stirred in our seats we wait with vague surmise
What haply comes that pleases or that palls.

Touched on the stand the thrice-struck baton calls,
Once more I watch the unfolding curtain rise,
I hear the exultant violins premise
The well-known tune that thrills me and enthralls.

Then trembling in my joy I see you flash
Before the footlights to the cymbals' clash,
With laughing lips, swift feet, and brilliant glance,

You, fair as heaven and as a rainbow bright,
You, queen of song and empress of the dance,
Flower of mine eyes, my love, my heart's delight!

THEODORE WRATISLAW
Caprices (1893)

MAQUILLAGE

The charm of rouge on fragile cheeks,
Pearl-powder, and, about the eyes,
The dark and lustrous Eastern dyes;
The floating odour that bespeaks
A scented boudoir and the doubtful night
Of alcoves curtained close against the light.

Gracile and creamy white and rose,
    Complexioned like the flower of dawn,
Her fleeting colours are as those
    That, from an April sky withdrawn,
Fade in a fragrant mist of tears away
When weeping noon leads on the altered day.

ARTHUR SYMONS
Silhouettes (2nd edition 1896)

THE WHITE STATUE

I love you, silent statue! for your sake
My songs in prayer upreach
Frail hands of flame-like speech
That some mauve-silver twilight you may wake!

I love you more than swallows love the south,
As sunflowers turn and turn
Towards the sun, I yearn
To press warm lips against your cold white mouth!

I love you more than scarlet skirted dawn,
At sight of whose spread wings
The great world wakes and sings;
Forgetful of the long, vague dark withdrawn.

I love you most at purple sunsetting:
When night with feverish eyes
Comes up the fading skies,
I love you with a passion past forgetting.

OLIVE CUSTANCE
Opals (1897)

BY THE STATUE OF KING CHARLES
AT CHARING CROSS

Sombre and rich, the skies;
Great glooms, and starry plains.
Gently the night wind sighs;
Else a vast silence reigns.

The splendid silence clings
Around me : and around
The saddest of all kings
Crowned, and again discrowned.

Comely and calm, he rides
Hard by his own Whitehall :
Only the night wind glides :
No crowds, nor rebels, brawl.

Gone, too, his Court : and yet,
The stars his courtiers are :
Stars in their stations set;
And every wandering star.

Alone he rides, alone,
The fair and fatal king :
Dark night is all his own,
That strange and solemn thing.

Which are more full of fate :
The stars; or those sad eyes?
Which are more still and great :
Those brows; or the dark skies?

Although his whole heart yearn
In passionate tragedy:
Never was face so stern
With sweet austerity.

Vanquished in life, his death
By beauty made amends:
The passing of his breath
Won his defeated ends.

Brief life, and hapless? Nay:
Through death, life grew sublime.
Speak after sentence? Yea:
And to the end of time.

Armoured he rides, his head
Bare to the stars of doom:
He triumphs now, the dead,
Beholding London's gloom.

Our wearier spirit faints,
Vexed in the world's employ:
His soul was of the saints;
And art to him was joy.

King, tried in fires of woe!
Men hunger for thy grace:
And through the night I go,
Loving thy mournful face.

Yet, when the city sleeps;
When all the cries are still:
The stars and heavenly deeps
Work out a perfect will.

LIONEL JOHNSON
Poems (1895)

LA GIOCONDA

LEONARDO DA VINCI
The Louvre

Historic, side-long, implicating eyes;
A smile of velvet's lustre on the cheek;
Calm lips the smile leads upward; hand that lies
Glowing and soft, the patience in its rest
Of cruelty that waits and doth not seek
For prey; a dusky forehead and a breast
Where twilight touches ripeness amorously:
Behind her, crystal rocks, a sea and skies
Of evanescent blue on cloud and creek;
Landscape that shines suppressive of its zest
For those vicissitudes by which men die.

MICHAEL FIELD
Sight and Song (1892)

TO MILTON, – BLIND

He who said suddenly, 'Let there be light!'
To thee the dark deliberately gave;
That those full eyes might undistracted be
By this beguiling show of sky and field,
This brilliance, that so lures us from the Truth.
He gave thee back original night, His own
Tremendous canvas, large and blank and free,
Where at each thought a star flashed out and sang.
O blinded with a special lightning, thou
Hadst once again the virgin Dark! and when
The pleasant flowery sight, which had deterred

Thine eyes from seeing, when this recent world
Was quite withdrawn; then burst upon thy view
The elder glory; space again in pangs,
And Eden odorous in the early mist,
That heaving watery plain that *was* the world;
Then the burned earth, and Christ coming in clouds.
Or rather a special leave to thee was given
By the high power, and thou with bandaged eyes
Wast guided through the glimmering camp of God.
Thy hand was taken by angels who patrol
The evening, or are sentries to the dawn,
Or pace the wide air everlastingly.
Thou wast admitted to the presence, and deep
Argument heardest, and the large design
That brings this world out of the woe to bliss.

STEPHEN PHILLIPS
Poems (1898)

PLATO IN LONDON

The pure flame of one taper fall
Over the old and comely page:
No harsher light disturb at all
This converse with a treasured sage.
Seemly, and fair, and of the best,
    If Plato be our guest,
    Should things befall.

Without, a world of noise and cold:
Here, the soft burning of the fire.
And Plato walks, where heavens unfold,
About the home of his desire.
From his own city of high things,
    He shows to us, and brings,
    Truth of fine gold.

The hours pass; and the fire burns low;
The clear flame dwindles into death:
Shut then the book with care; and so,
Take leave of Plato, with hushed breath:
A little, by the falling gleams,
    Tarry the gracious dreams:
    And they too go.

Lean from the window to the air:
Hear London's voice upon the night!
Thou hast bold converse with things rare:
Look now upon another sight!
The calm stars, in their living skies:
    And then, these surging cries,
    This restless glare!

That starry music, starry fire,
High above all our noise and glare:
The image of our long desire,
The beauty, and the strength, are there.
And Plato's thought lives, true and clear,
    In as august a sphere:
    Perchance, far higher.

LIONEL JOHNSON
Poems (1895)

THE THREE MUSICIANS

Along the path that skirts the wood,
    The three musicians wend their way,
Pleased with their thoughts, each other's mood,
    Franz Himmel's latest roundelay,
The morning's work, a new-found theme, their breakfast
    and the summer day.

Aubrey Beardsley

One's a soprano, lightly frocked
  In cool, white muslin that just shows
Her brown silk stockings gaily clocked,
  Plump arms and elbows tipped with rose,
And frills of petticoats and things, and outlines as the warm
  wind blows.

Beside her a slim, gracious boy
  Hastens to mend her tresses' fall,
And dies her favour to enjoy,
  And dies for *réclame* and recall
At Paris and St Petersburg, Vienna and St James's Hall.

The third's a Polish Pianist
  With big engagements everywhere,
A light heart and an iron wrist,
  And shocks and shoals of yellow hair,
And fingers that can trill on sixths and fill beginners with
  despair.

The three musicians stroll along
  And pluck the ears of ripened corn,
Break into odds and ends of song,
  And mock the woods with Siegfried's horn,
And fill the air with Gluck, and fill the tweeded tourist's soul
  with scorn.

The Polish genius lags behind,
  And, with some poppies in his hand,
Picks out the strings and wood and wind
  Of an imaginary band,
Enchanted that for once his men obey his beat and
  understand.

The charming cantatrice reclines
    And rests a moment where she sees
Her château's roof that hotly shines
    Amid the dusky summer trees,
And fans herself, half shuts her eyes, and smoothes the
  frock about her knees.

The gracious boy is at her feet,
    And weighs his courage with his chance;
His fears soon melt in noonday heat.
    The tourist gives a furious glance,
Red as his guide-book grows, moves on, and offers up a
  prayer for France.

AUBREY BEARDSLEY
In *The Savoy* (1896)

THE FIDDLER OF DOONEY

When I play on my fiddle in Dooney,
Folk dance like a wave of the sea;
My cousin is priest in Kilvarnet,
My brother in Moharabuiee.

I passed my brother and cousin:
They read in their books of prayers;
I read in my book of songs
I bought at the Sligo fair.

When we come at the end of time,
To Peter sitting in state,
He will smile on the three old spirits,
But call me first through the gate;

For the good are always the merry,
    Save by an evil chance,
And the merry love the fiddle
And the merry love to dance:

And when the folk there spy me,
    They will all come up to me,
With 'Here is the fiddler of Dooney!'
And dance like a wave of the sea.

W. B. YEATS
The Wind Among the Reeds (1899)

JAVANESE DANCERS

Twitched strings, the clang of metal, beaten drums,
    Dull, shrill, continuous, disquieting;
And now the stealthy dancer comes
    Undulantly with cat-like steps that cling;

Smiling between her painted lids a smile,
    Motionless, unintelligible, she twines
    Her fingers into mazy lines,
Twining her scarves across them all the while.

One, two, three, four step forth, and, to and fro,
    Delicately and imperceptibly,
Now swaying gently in a row,
    Now interthreading slow and rhythmically,

Still with fixed eyes, monotonously still,
    Mysteriously, with smiles inanimate,
    With lingering feet that undulate,
With sinuous fingers, spectral hands that thrill,

The little amber-coloured dancers move,
    Like little painted figures on a screen,
    Or phantom-dancers haply seen
Among the shadows of a magic grove.

ARTHUR SYMONS
Silhouettes (2nd edition 1896)

2. *London! London! Our Delight*

IT was inevitable that artists and writers who subscribed to a theory which placed the artificial above the natural should come to paint and write of the city, seeing it as a central symbol of man's shaping of his world. This love of artificial things is in a sense a complete reversal of the Romantic idea of the beauty of Nature and the corrupting influence of man. Wits like Whistler and Wilde delighted in standing this familiar idea on its head and asserting that Nature imitates Art. When a woman said that a landscape reminded her of his work, Whistler replied, 'Yes madam, Nature is creeping up.' And Vivian in Wilde's 'The Decay of Lying' insists that 'the extraordinary change that has taken place in the climate of London during the past ten years is entirely due to a particular school of Art'. Beardsley, borrowing these ideas and the manner of Beerbohm, wrote with some glee in the *New Review* that

London will soon be resplendent with advertisements, and against a leaden sky skysigns will trace their formal arabesque. Beauty has laid siege to the city, and telegraph wires shall no longer be the sole joy of our aesthetic perceptions.[1]

Symons put a less extreme case more calmly in the preface to the second edition of his *Silhouettes* (1896).

There is no necessary difference in artistic value between a good poem about a flower in the hedge and a good poem about the scent in a sachet. I am always charmed to read beautiful poems about nature in the country. Only, personally, I prefer town to country; and in the town we have to find for ourselves, as best we

1. Quoted by Stanley Weintraub in *Aubrey Beardsley*, 1967.

may, the *décor* which is the town equivalent of the great natural *décor* of fields and hills. Here it is that artificiality comes in; and if any one sees no beauty in the effects of artificial light, in all the variable, most human, and yet most factitious town landscape, I can only pity him, and go on my own way.

Whether the influence to write urban poetry came, as Richard Le Gallienne suggested, from Robert Buchanan's *London Poems* (1866), or from French ideas, or from the vast influx of people into the towns, or a combination of these and other reasons, the popularity of the subject is demonstrated by W. E. Henley's *London Types* (1898), and *London Voluntaries* (1893), Laurence Binyon's two series of *London Lyrics* (1896 and 1899), Ernest Rhys's *A London Rose* (1894), John Davidson's *Fleet Street Eclogues* (1893), and Arthur Symons's *London Nights* (1895), to name only those books whose titles indicate their interest.

Twentieth-century poetry has tended to be predominantly urban, though the Georgians for example would prefer semi-rural subjects, and Eliot acknowledged his debt to 'nineties writers (see section 3). And though Yeats, unlike his friends, rarely put London into his poems, he understood the significance of the city; for it occurs in his later poems, transformed into the 'holy city of Byzantium', where Yeats comes, to borrow Beerbohm's words (see section 1), 'nearest to God' in that climactic use of the idea of the superiority of the artificial to the natural:

> gather me
> Into the artifice of eternity.

A BALLAD OF LONDON

Ah, London! London! our delight,
Great flower that opens but at night,
Great City of the Midnight Sun,
Whose day begins when day is done.

Lamp after lamp against the sky
Opens a sudden beaming eye,
Leaping alight on either hand,
The iron lilies of the Strand.

Like dragonflies, the hansoms hover,
With jewelled eyes, to catch the lover;
The streets are full of lights and loves,
Soft gowns, and flutter of soiled doves.

The human moths about the light
Dash and cling close in dazed delight,
And burn and laugh, the world and wife,
For this is London, this is life!

Upon thy petals butterflies,
But at thy root, some say, there lies
A world of weeping trodden things,
Poor worms that have not eyes or wings.

From out corruption of their woe
Springs this bright flower that charms us so,
Men die and rot deep out of sight
To keep this jungle-flower bright.

Paris and London, World-Flowers twain
Wherewith the World-Tree blooms again,
Since Time hath gathered Babylon,
And withered Rome still withers on.

Sidon and Tyre were such as ye,
How bright they shone upon the Tree!
But Time hath gathered, both are gone,
And no man sails to Babylon.

Ah, London! London! our delight,
For thee, too, the eternal night,
And Circe Paris hath no charm
To stay Time's unrelenting arm.

Time and his moths shall eat up all.
Your chiming towers proud and tall
He shall most utterly abase,
And set a desert in their place.

RICHARD LE GALLIENNE
Robert Louis Stevenson: an Elegy, and Other Poems (1895)

LONDON

Athwart the sky a lowly sigh
    From west to east the sweet wind carried;
The sun stood still on Primrose Hill;
    His light in all the city tarried:
The clouds on viewless columns bloomed
Like smouldering lilies unconsumed.

'Oh sweetheart, see! how shadowy,
    Of some occult magician's rearing,
Or swung in space of heaven's grace
    Dissolving, dimly reappearing,

Afloat upon ethereal tides
St Paul's above the city rides!'

A rumour broke through the thin smoke
   Enwreathing abbey, tower, and palace,
The parks, the squares, the thoroughfares,
   The million-peopled lanes and alleys,
An ever-muttering prisoned storm,
The heart of London beating warm.

JOHN DAVIDSON
Ballads and Songs (1894)

IMPRESSION DE NUIT

LONDON

See what a mass of gems the city wears
Upon her broad live bosom! row on row
Rubies and emeralds and amethysts glow.
See! that huge circle like a necklace, stares
With thousands of bold eyes to heaven, and dares
The golden stars to dim the lamps below,
And in the mirror of the mire I know
The moon has left her image unawares.

That's the great town at night: I see her breasts,
Pricked out with lamps they stand like huge black towers,
I think they move! I hear her panting breath.
And that's her head where the tiara rests.
And in her brain, through lanes as dark as death,
Men creep like thoughts. . . . The lamps are like pale
   flowers.

LORD ALFRED DOUGLAS
The City of the Soul (1899)

SUNSET IN THE CITY

Above the town a monstrous wheel is turning,
    With glowing spokes of red,
Low in the west its fiery axle burning;
    And, lost amid the spaces overhead,
A vague white moth, the moon, is fluttering.

Above the town an azure sea is flowing,
    'Mid long peninsulas of shining sand,
From opal unto pearl the moon is growing,
    Dropped like a shell upon the changing strand.

Within the town the streets grow strange and haunted,
    And, dark against the western lakes of green,
The buildings change to temples, and unwonted
    Shadows and sounds creep in where day has been.

Within the town, the lamps of sin are flaring,
    Poor foolish men that know not what ye are!
Tired traffic still upon his feet is faring –
    Two lovers meet and kiss and watch a star.

RICHARD LE GALLIENNE
English Poems (1892)

CITY NIGHTS

I. IN THE TRAIN

The train through the night of the town,
    Through a blackness broken in twain
        By the sudden finger of streets;
Lights, red, yellow, and brown,
    From curtain and window-pane,
        The flashing eyes of the streets.

Night, and the rush of the train,
　　A cloud of smoke through the town,
　　　Scaring the life of the streets;
And the leap of the heart again,
　　Out into the night, and down
　　　The dazzling vista of streets!

2. IN THE TEMPLE

The grey and misty night,
　　Slim trees that hold the night among
　　Their branches, and, along
The vague Embankment, light on light.

The sudden, racing lights!
　　I can just hear, distinct, aloof,
　　The gaily clattering hoof
Beating the rhythm of festive nights.

The gardens to the weeping moon
　　Sigh back the breath of tears.
　　O the refrain of years on years
'Neath the weeping moon!

ARTHUR SYMONS
Silhouettes (2nd edition 1896)

A NORTHERN SUBURB

Nature selects the longest way,
　　And winds about in tortuous grooves;
A thousand years the oaks decay;
　　The wrinkled glacier hardly moves.

But here the whetted fangs of change
　　Daily devour the old demesne –
The busy farm, the quiet grange,
　　The wayside inn, the village green.

In gaudy yellow brick and red,
　　With rooting pipes, like creepers rank,
The shoddy terraces o'erspread
　　Meadow, and garth, and daisied bank.

With shelves for rooms the houses crowd,
　　Like draughty cupboards in a row –
Ice-chests when wintry winds are loud,
　　Ovens when summer breezes blow.

Roused by the fee'd policeman's knock,
　　And sad that day should come again,
Under the stars the workmen flock
　　In haste to reach the workmen's train.

For here dwell those who must fulfil
　　Dull tasks in uncongenial spheres,
Who toil through dread of coming ill,
　　And not with hope of happier years –

The lowly folk who scarcely dare
　　Conceive themselves perhaps misplaced,
Whose prize for unremitting care
　　Is only not to be disgraced.

JOHN DAVIDSON
New Ballads (1897)

LONDON VOLUNTARIES

3

Scherzando

Down through the ancient Strand
The spirit of October, mild and boon
And sauntering, takes his way
This golden end of afternoon,
As though the corn stood yellow in all the land
And the ripe apples dropped to the harvest-moon.

Lo! the round sun, half-down the western slope —
Seen as along an unglazed telescope —
Lingers and lolls, loth to be done with day:
Gifting the long, lean, lanky street
And its abounding confluences of being
With aspects generous and bland;
Making a thousand harnesses to shine
As with new ore from some enchanted mine,
And every horse's coat so full of sheen
He looks new-tailored, and every 'bus feels clean,
And never a hansom but is worth the feeing;
And every jeweller within the pale
Offers a real Arabian Night for sale;
And even the roar
Of the strong streams of toil, that pause and pour
Eastward and westward, sounds suffused —
Seems as it were bemused
And blurred, and like the speech
Of lazy seas on a lotus-haunted beach —
With this enchanted lustrousness,
This mellow magic, that (as a man's caress

Brings back to some faded face, beloved before,
A heavenly shadow of the grace it wore
Ere the poor eyes were minded to beseech)
Old things transfigures, and you hail and bless
Their looks of long-lapsed loveliness once more:
Till Clement's, angular and cold and staid,
Gleams forth in glamour's very stuffs arrayed;
And Bride's, her aëry, unsubstantial charm
Through flight on flight of springing, soaring stone
Grown flushed and warm,
Laughs into life full-mooded and fresh-blown;
And the high majesty of Paul's
Uplifts a voice of living light, and calls –
Calls to his millions to behold and see
How goodly this his London Town can be!

For earth and sky and air
Are golden everywhere,
And golden with a gold so suave and fine
The looking on it lifts the heart like wine.
Trafalgar Square
(The fountains volleying golden glaze)
Shines like an angel-market. High aloft
Over his couchant Lions in a haze
Shimmering and bland and soft,
A dust of chrysoprase,
Our Sailor takes the golden gaze
Of the saluting sun, and flames superb
As once he flamed it on his ocean round.
The dingy dreariness of the picture-place,
Turned very nearly bright,
Takes on a luminous transiency of grace,
And shows no more a scandal to the ground.
The very blind man pottering on the kerb,

Among the posies and the ostrich feathers
And the rude voices touched with all the weathers
Of the long, varying year,
Shares in the universal alms of light.
The windows, with their fleeting, flickering fires,
The height and spread of frontage shining sheer,
The quiring signs, the rejoicing roofs and spires –
'Tis El Dorado – El Dorado plain,
The Golden City! And when a girl goes by,
Look! as she turns her glancing head,
A call of gold is floated from her ear!
Golden, all golden! In a golden glory,
Long-lapsing down a golden coasted sky,
The day not dies but seems
Dispersed in wafts and drifts of gold, and shed
Upon a past of golden song and story
And memories of gold and golden dreams.

W. E. HENLEY
Poems (1898)

4

Largo e mesto

Out of the poisonous East,
Over a continent of blight,
Like a maleficent Influence released
From the most squalid cellarage of hell,
The Wind-Fiend, the abominable –
The Hangman Wind that tortures temper and light –
Comes slouching, sullen and obscene,
Hard on the skirts of the embittered night;
And in a cloud unclean
Of excremental humours, roused to strife
By the operation of some ruinous change

Wherever his evil mandate run and range
Into a dire intensity of life,
A craftsman at his bench, he settles down
To the grim job of throttling London Town.

So, by a jealous lightlessness beset
That might have oppressed the dragons of old time
Crunching and groping in the abysmal slime,
A cave of cut-throat thoughts and villainous dreams,
Hag-rid and crying with cold and dirt and wet,
The afflicted City, prone from mark to mark
In shameful occultation, seems
A nightmare labyrinthine, dim and drifting,
With wavering gulfs and antic heights, and shifting,
Rent in the stuff of a material dark,
Wherein the lamplight, scattered and sick and pale,
Shows like the leper's living blotch of bale:
Uncoiling monstrous into street on street
Paven with perils, teeming with mischance,
Where man and beast go blindfold and in dread,
Working with oaths and threats and faltering feet
Somewhither in the hideousness ahead;
Working through wicked airs and deadly dews
That make the laden robber grin askance
At the good places in his black romance,
And the poor, loitering harlot rather choose
Go pinched and pined to bed
Than lurk and shiver and curse her wretched way
From arch to arch, scouting some threepenny prey.

Forgot his dawns and far-flushed afterglows,
His green garlands and windy eyots forgot,
The old Father-River flows,

His watchfires cores of menace in the gloom,
As he came oozing from the Pit, and bore,
Sunk in his filthily transfigured sides,
Shoals of dishonoured dead to tumble and rot
In the squalor of the universal shore:
His voices sounding through the gruesome air
As from the Ferry where the Boat of Doom
With her blaspheming cargo reels and rides:
The while his children, the brave ships,
No more adventurous and fair,
Nor tripping it light of heel as home-bound brides,
But infamously enchanted,
Huddle together in the foul eclipse,
Or feel their course by inches desperately,
As through a tangle of alleys murder-haunted,
From sinister reach to reach out – out – to sea.

And Death the while –
Death with his well-worn, lean, professional smile,
Death in his threadbare working trim –
Comes to your bedside, unannounced and bland,
And with expert, inevitable hand
Feels at your windpipe, fingers you in the lung,
Or flicks the clot well into the labouring heart:
Thus signifying unto old and young,
However hard of mouth or wild of whim,
'Tis time – 'tis time by his ancient watch – to part
From books and women and talk and drink and art.
And you go humbly after him
To a mean suburban lodging: on the way
To what or where
Not Death, who is old and very wise, can say:
And you – how should you care

So long as, unreclaimed of hell,
The Wind-Fiend, the insufferable,
Thus vicious and thus patient, sits him down
To the black job of burking London Town?

W. E. HENLEY
Poems (1898)

IN THE ISLE OF DOGS

While the water-wagon's ringing showers
Sweetened the dust with a woodland smell,
'Past noon, past noon, two sultry hours,'
Drowsily fell
From the schoolhouse clock
In the Isle of Dogs by Millwall Dock.

Mirrored in shadowy windows draped
With ragged net or half-drawn blind
Bowsprits, masts, exactly shaped
To woo or fight the wind,
Like monitors of guilt
By strength and beauty sent,
Disgraced the shameful houses built
To furnish rent.

From the pavements and the roofs
In shimmering volumes wound
The wrinkled heat;
Distant hammers, wheels and hoofs,
A turbulent pulse of sound,
Southward obscurely beat,
The only utterance of the afternoon,
Till on a sudden in the silent street

70

An organ-man drew up and ground
The Old Hundredth tune.

Forthwith the pillar of cloud that hides the past
Burst into flame,
Whose alchemy transmuted house and mast,
Street, dockyard, pier and pile:
By magic sound the Isle of Dogs became
A northern isle –
A green isle like a beryl set
In a wine-coloured sea,
Shadowed by mountains where a river met
The ocean's arm extended royally.

There also in the evening on the shore
An old man ground the Old Hundredth tune,
An old enchanter steeped in human lore,
Sad-eyed, with whitening beard, and visage lank:
Not since and not before,
Under the sunset or the mellowing moon,
Has any hand of man's conveyed
Such meaning in the turning of a crank.

Sometimes he played
As if his box had been
An organ in an abbey richly lit;
For when the dark invaded day's demesne,
And the sun set in crimson and in gold;
When idlers swarmed upon the esplanade,
And a late steamer wheeling towards the quay
Struck founts of silver from the darkling sea,
The solemn tune arose and shook and rolled
Above the throng,
Above the hum and tramp and bravely knit
All hearts in common memories of song.

Sometimes he played at speed;
Then the Old Hundredth like a devil's mass
Instinct with evil thought and evil deed,
Rang out in anguish and remorse. Alas!
That men must know both Heaven and Hell!
Sometimes the melody
Sang with the murmuring surge;
And with the winds would tell
Of peaceful graves and of the passing bell.
Sometimes it pealed across the bay
A high triumphal dirge,
A dirge
For the departing undefeated day.

A noble tune, a high becoming mate
Of the capped mountains and the deep broad firth;
A simple tune and great,
The fittest utterance of the voice of earth.

JOHN DAVIDSON
The Last Ballad (1899)

IMPRESSION

The pink and black of silk and lace,
    Flushed in the rosy-golden glow
Of lamplight on her lifted face;
Powder and wig, and pink and lace,

And those pathetic eyes of hers;
    But all the London footlights know
The little plaintive smile that stirs
The shadow in those eyes of hers.

Outside, the dreary church-bell tolled,
　　The London Sunday faded slow;
Ah, what is this? what wings unfold
In this miraculous rose of gold?

ARTHUR SYMONS
Silhouettes (2nd edition 1896)

AT THE CAVOUR

Wine, the red coals, the flaring gas,
　　Bring out a brighter tone in cheeks
That learn at home before the glass
　　The flush that eloquently speaks.

The blue-grey smoke of cigarettes
　　Curls from the lessening ends that glow;
The men are thinking of the bets,
　　The women of the debts, they owe.

Then their eyes meet, and in their eyes
　　The accustomed smile comes up to call,
A look half miserably wise,
　　Half heedlessly ironical.

ARTHUR SYMONS
Silhouettes (2nd edition 1896)

ETCHINGS

3

AT THE EMPIRE

The low and soft luxurious promenade,
Electric-light, pile-carpet, the device
Of gilded mirrors that repeat you thrice;
The crowd that lounges, strolls from yard to yard;

The calm and brilliant Circes who retard
Your passage with the skirts and rouge that spice
The changeless programme of insipid vice,
And stun you with a languid strange regard;

Ah! what are these, the perfume and the glow,
The ballet that coruscates down below,
The glittering songstress and the comic stars,

Ah! what are these, although we sit withdrawn
Above our sparkling tumblers and cigars,
To us so like to perish with a yawn?

THEODORE WRATISLAW
Orchids (1896)

3. *London Types*

LONDON TYPES

THREE things combined to make London types a popular subject for poetry. First, the interest in London itself (see the previous section; though the Edinburgh of Henley's hospital, or the Paris of Symons's music-hall would do as well); second, the tradition of the dramatic monologue and depiction of character, which the poets learned from Browning and Tennyson (Symons's first book had been *An Introduction to the Study of Browning*, 1886) and which they passed on to Pound and Eliot; third, the rising interest in the rights of the ordinary man, as exemplified by the socialist movements. Though present in some novels and factual reports, these types had tended to be unacceptable in poetry, only appearing transformed into the sentimental heroes and heroines of poets like G. R. Sims. And they were not always acceptable in prose. W. T. Stead had published a series of articles called 'The Maiden Tribute of Modern Babylon', where he told how he had been able to buy for £5 a girl of just over thirteen, ostensibly for vicious purposes. His aim, in which he was successful, was to secure the passing of the Criminal Law Amendment Bill (1885), but he so shocked the nation that he was gaoled for three months, and W. H. Smith refused to sell the paper which carried his articles. Smith's also refused to sell George Moore's *Esther Waters* (1894), a novel which describes the difficult life of a servant girl.

Now both the actions and the voice of the ordinary man began to find a place in poetry; once more back to a language more nearly that really used by men. T. S. Eliot wrote in the preface to Maurice Lindsay's *John Davidson: a Selection of his Poems* (1961) that

Thirty Bob a Week seems to me the only poem in which Davidson freed himself completely from the poetic diction of English verse of his time (just as *Non Sum Qualis Eram* seems to me the one poem in which, by a slight shift of rhythm, Ernest Dowson freed himself). But I am sure that I found inspiration in the content of the poem, and in the complete fitness of content and idiom: for I also had a good many dingy urban images to reveal. Davidson had a great theme, and also found an idiom which elicited the greatness of the theme, which endowed this thirty-bob-a-week clerk with a dignity that would not have appeared if a more conventional poetic diction had been employed. The personage that Davidson created in this poem has haunted me all my life, and the poem is to me a great poem for ever.

Others were finding this idiom: Kipling, for example, or Henley, who was not only writing his *London Types* but also helping throughout the 'nineties to compile and edit a dictionary of *Slang and its Analogues*.

Some held aloof from these matters and from social upheavals. Yeats wrote that 'we poets continued to write verse and read it out at "The Cheshire Cheese", convinced that to take part in such movements would be only less disgraceful than to write for the newspapers'.[1]

Like the city itself, dancers were both symbol and substance, and Symons, an ardent admirer of dancers in the flesh, also states very clearly the symbolic role of the dancer, which is seen also in the poems of Davidson and Binyon. Again it is Yeats who, much later, makes fullest use of this symbol, as in 'Byzantium'.

1. *Oxford Book of Modern Verse.*

THIRTY BOB A WEEK

I couldn't touch a stop and turn a screw,
 And set the blooming world a-work for me,
Like such as cut their teeth – I hope, like you –
 On the handle of a skeleton gold key;
I cut mine on a leek, which I eat it every week:
 I'm a clerk at thirty bob as you can see.

But I don't allow it's luck and all a toss;
 There's no such thing as being starred and crossed;
It's just the power of some to be a boss,
 And the bally power of others to be bossed:
I face the music, sir; you bet I ain't a cur;
 Strike me lucky if I don't believe I'm lost!

For like a mole I journey in the dark,
 A-travelling along the underground
From my Pillar'd Halls and broad Suburbean Park,
 To come the daily dull official round;
And home again at night with my pipe all alight,
 A-scheming how to count ten bob a pound.

And it's often very cold and very wet,
 And my missis stitches towels for a hunks;
And the Pillar'd Halls is half of it to let –
 Three rooms about the size of travelling trunks.
And we cough, my wife and I, to dislocate a sigh,
 When the noisy little kids are in their bunks.

But you never hear her do a growl or whine,
    For she's made of flint and roses, very odd;
And I've got to cut my meaning rather fine,
    Or I'd blubber, for I'm made of greens and sod:
So p'r'aps we are in Hell for all that I can tell,
    And lost and damn'd and served up hot to God.

I ain't blaspheming, Mr Silver-tongue;
    I'm saying things a bit beyond your art:
Of all the rummy starts you ever sprung,
    Thirty bob a week's the rummiest start!
With your science and your books and your the'ries about
    spooks,
    Did you ever hear of looking in your heart?

I didn't mean your pocket, Mr, no:
    I mean that having children and a wife,
With thirty bob on which to come and go,
    Isn't dancing to the tabor and the fife:
When it doesn't make you drink, by Heaven! it makes you
    think,
    And notice curious items about life.

I step into my heart and there I meet
    A god-almighty devil singing small,
Who would like to shout and whistle in the street,
    And squelch the passers flat against the wall;
If the whole world was a cake he had the power to take,
    He would take it, ask for more, and eat it all.

And I meet a sort of simpleton beside,
    The kind that life is always giving beans;
With thirty bob a week to keep a bride
    He fell in love and married in his teens:
At thirty bob he stuck; but he knows it isn't luck:
    He knows the seas are deeper than tureens.

And the god-almighty devil and the fool
    That meet me in the High Street on the strike,
When I walk about my heart a-gathering wool,
    Are my good and evil angels if you like.
And both of them together in every kind of weather
    Ride me like a double-seated bike.

That's rough a bit and needs its meaning curled.
    But I have a high old hot un in my mind –
A most engrugious notion of the world,
    That leaves your lightning 'rithmetic behind:
I give it at a glance when I say 'There ain't no chance,
    Nor nothing of the lucky-lottery kind.'

And it's this way that I make it out to be:
    No fathers, mothers, countries, climates – none;
Not Adam was responsible for me,
    Nor society, nor systems, nary one:
A little sleeping seed, I woke – I did, indeed –
    A million years before the blooming sun.

I woke because I thought the time had come;
    Beyond my will there was no other cause;
And everywhere I found myself at home,
    Because I chose to be the thing I was;
And in whatever shape of mollusc or of ape
    I always went according to the laws.

I was the love that chose my mother out;
    I joined two lives and from the union burst;
My weakness and my strength without a doubt
    Are mine alone for ever from the first:
It's just the very same with a difference in the name
    As 'Thy will be done.' You say it if you durst!

They say it daily up and down the land
　　As easy as you take a drink, it's true;
But the difficultest go to understand,
　　And the difficultest job a man can do,
Is to come it brave and meek with thirty bob a week,
　　And feel that that's the proper thing for you.

It's a naked child against a hungry wolf;
　　It's playing bowls upon a splitting wreck;
It's walking on a string across a gulf
　　With millstones fore-and-aft about your neck;
But the thing is daily done by many and many a one;
　　And we fall, face forward, fighting, on the deck.

JOHN DAVIDSON
Ballads and Songs (1894)

TOMMY

I went into a public-'ouse to get a pint o' beer,
The publican 'e up an' sez, 'We serve no red-coats here.'
The girls be'ind the bar they laughed an' giggled fit to die,
I outs into the street again an' to myself sez I:
　　O it's Tommy this, an' Tommy that, an' 'Tommy,
　　　　go away';
　　But it's 'Thank you, Mister Atkins,' when the band
　　　　begins to play,
　　The band begins to play, my boys, the band begins to
　　　　play,
　　O it's 'Thank you, Mister Atkins,' when the band
　　　　begins to play.

I went into a theatre as sober as could be,
They gave a drunk civilian room, but 'adn't none for me;

They sent me to the gallery or round the music-'alls,
But when it comes to fightin', Lord! they'll shove me in the
stalls!
    For it's Tommy this, an' Tommy that, an' 'Tommy,
      wait outside';
    But it's 'Special train for Atkins' when the trooper's
      on the tide,
    The troopship's on the tide, my boys, the troopship's
      on the tide,
    O it's 'Special train for Atkins' when the trooper's on
      the tide.

Yes, makin' mock o' uniforms that guard you while you
sleep
Is cheaper than them uniforms, an' they're starvation
cheap;
An' hustlin' drunken soldiers, when they're goin' large a
bit
Is five times better business than paradin' in full kit.
    Then it's Tommy this, an' Tommy that, an'
      'Tommy, 'ow's yer soul?'
    But it's 'Thin red line of 'eroes' when the drums begin
      to roll,
    The drums begin to roll, my boys, the drums begin to
      to roll,
    O it's 'Thin red line of 'eroes' when the drums begin
      to roll.

We aren't no thin red 'eroes, nor we aren't no blackguards
too,
But single men in barricks, most remarkable like you;
An' if sometimes our conduck isn't all your fancy paints,
Why, single men in barricks don't grow into plaster saints;
    While it's Tommy this, an' Tommy that, an' 'Tommy,
      fall be'ind,'

But it's 'Please to walk in front, sir,' when there's
    trouble in the wind,
There's trouble in the wind, my boys, there's trouble
    in the wind,
  O it's 'Please to walk in front, sir,' when there's
    trouble in the wind.

You talk o' better food for us, an' schools, an' fires, an' all:
We'll wait for extry rations if you treat us rational.
Don't mess about the cook-room slops, but prove it to our
  face
The Widow's Uniform is not the soldier-man's disgrace.
    For it's Tommy this, an' Tommy that, an' 'Chuck him
      out, the brute!'
    But it's 'Saviour of 'is country' when the guns begin to
      shoot;
    An' it's Tommy this, an' Tommy that, an' anything
      you please;
    An' Tommy ain't a bloomin' fool – you bet that
      Tommy sees!

RUDYARD KIPLING
Barrack-Room Ballads (1892)

ANY BAR

Though, if you ask her name, she says ELISE,
Being plain ELIZABETH, e'en let it pass,
And own that, if her aspirates take their ease,
She ever makes a point, in washing glass,
Handling the engine, turning taps for tots,
And countering change, and scorning what men say,
Of posing as a dove among the pots,
Nor often gives her dignity away.

Her head's a work of art, and, if her eyes
Be tired and ignorant, she has a waist;
Cheaply the mode she shadows; and she tries
From penny novels to amend her taste;
   And, having mopped the zinc for certain years,
   And faced the gas, she fades and disappears.

W. E. HENLEY
London Types (1898)

IN HOSPITAL

9

LADY-PROBATIONER

Some three, or five, or seven, and thirty years;
A Roman nose; a dimpling double-chin;
Dark eyes and shy that, ignorant of sin,
Are yet acquainted, it would seem, with tears;
A comely shape; a slim, high-coloured hand,
Graced, rather oddly, with a signet ring;
A bashful air, becoming everything;
A well-bred silence always at command.
Her plain print gown, prim cap, and bright steel chain
Look out of place on her, and I remain
Absorbed in her, as in a pleasant mystery.
Quick, skilful, quiet, soft in speech and touch . . .
'Do you like nursing?' 'Yes, Sir, very much.'
Somehow, I rather think she has a history.

W. E. HENLEY
Poems (1898)

IN HOSPITAL

10

STAFF-NURSE: NEW STYLE

Blue-eyed and bright of face but waning fast
Into the sere of virginal decay,
I view her as she enters, day by day,
As a sweet sunset almost overpast.
Kindly and calm, patrician to the last,
Superbly falls her gown of sober gray,
And on her chignon's elegant array
The plainest cap is somehow touched with caste.
She talks BEETHOVEN; frowns disapprobation
At BALZAC's name, sighs it at 'poor GEORGE SAND's';
Knows that she has exceeding pretty hands;
Speaks Latin with a right accentuation;
And gives at need (as one who understands)
Draught, counsel, diagnosis, exhortation.

W. E. HENLEY
Poems (1898)

HOLIDAY AT HAMPTON COURT

Scales of pearly cloud inlay
    North and south the turquoise sky,
While the diamond lamp of day
    Quenchless burns, and time on high
A moment halts upon his way
    Bidding noon again good-bye.

Gaffers, gammers, huzzies, louts,
   Couples, gangs, and families
Sprawling, shake, with Babel-shouts
   Bluff King Hal's funereal trees;
And eddying groups of stare-abouts
   Quiz the sandstone Hercules.

When their tongues and tempers tire,
   Harry and his little lot
Condescendingly admire
   Lozenge-bed and crescent-plot,
Aglow with links of azure fire,
   Pansy and forget-me-not.

Where the emerald shadows rest
   In the lofty woodland aisle,
Chaffing lovers quaintly dressed
   Chase and double many a mile,
Indifferent exiles in the west
   Making love in cockney style.

Now the echoing palace fills;
   Men and women, girls and boys
Trample past the swords and frills,
   Kings and Queens and trulls and toys;
Or listening loll on window-sills,
   Happy amateurs of noise!

That for pictured rooms of state!
   Out they hurry, wench and knave,
Where beyond the palace-gate
   Dusty legions swarm and rave,
With laughter, shriek, inane debate,
   Kentish fire and comic stave.

Voices from the river call;
    Organs hammer tune on tune;
Larks triumphant over all
    Herald twilight coming soon,
For as the sun begins to fall
    Near the zenith gleams the moon.

JOHN DAVIDSON
The Last Ballad (1899)

IN THE SEASON

Her insolent carriage shines down Rotten Row,
Her beauty shaded from the sun of June
Outblazes even the dazzling afternoon;
Her heart is hard and hot with triumph; though
Her eyelids droop too languid to bestow
A glance upon the crowd that drives or stands,
She feels the reins of conquest in her hands,
Exulting in the senses' overthrow.

The champing horses bear her down the mile,
And as all eyes go after her a smile
Dawns and is gone upon the clear-cut face:

She leans back on the cushions to recall
The night's long list of dinner, theatre, ball,
In languors of premeditated grace.

THEODORE WRATISLAW
Caprices (1893)

HAMMERSMITH

'LIZA's *old man*'s perhaps a little *shady*,
'LIZA's *old woman*'s prone to *booze* and cringe;
But 'LIZA deems herself *a perfect lady*,
And proves it in her feathers and her fringe.
For 'LIZA has a *bloke* her heart to cheer,
With *pearlies* and a *barrer* and a *jack*,
So all the vegetables of the year
Are duly represented on her back.
Her boots are sacrifices to her hats,
Which knock you speechless – *like a load of bricks!*
Her summer velvets dazzle WANSTEAD FLATS,
And cost, at times, a good eighteen-and-six.
    Withal, outside the gay and giddy whirl,
      'LIZA's a stupid, straight, hard-working girl.

W. E. HENLEY
London Types (1898)

PAPILLONS DU PAVÉ

A butterfly, a queer red thing,
Comes drifting idly down the street:
Ah, do not now the cool leaves swing,
That you must brave the city's heat?

A butterfly, a poet vain,
Whose life is weeping in his mind,
And all the dreaming of his brain
Is blighted by the dusty wind.

A painted butterfly sits there,
Who sickens of the café chaff;
And down the sultry evening air
She flings her sudden weary laugh.

VINCENT O'SULLIVAN
Poems (1896)

NORA ON THE PAVEMENT

As Nora on the pavement
Dances, and she entrances the grey hour
Into the laughing circle of her power,
The magic circle of her glances,
As Nora dances on the midnight pavement;

Petulant and bewildered,
Thronging desires and longing looks recur,
And memorably re-incarnate her,
As I remember that old longing,
A footlight fancy, petulant and bewildered;

There where the ballet circles,
See her, but ah! not free her from the race
Of glittering lines that link and interlace;
This colour now, now that, may be her,
In the bright web of those harmonious circles.

But what are these dance-measures,
Leaping and joyous, keeping time alone
With Life's capricious rhythm, and all her own,
Life's rhythm and hers, long sleeping,
That wakes, and knows not why, in these dance-measures?

It is the very Nora;
Child, and most blithe, and wild as any elf,
And innocently spendthrift of herself,
And guileless and most unbeguiled,
Herself at last, leaps free the very Nora.

It is the soul of Nora,
Living at last, and giving forth to the night,
Bird-like, the burden of its own delight,
All its desire, and all the joy of living,
In that blithe madness of the soul of Nora.

ARTHUR SYMONS
Silhouettes (2nd edition 1896)

MARI'S SATURDAY NIGHTS

2

OCTOBER: THE PHILOSOPHY OF THE PAVEMENT

What if my face be pale, she said:
    For I can buy it colour.
What if my virtue's frail, she said:
    Since life gets dull and duller,
Let it go fast and faster, till I'm dead!

And if I die so soon, she said,
    Far better, dead and buried,
Than living this wild life, she said,
    Where women are so wearied,
Upon the endless pavement that they tread.

And if God is so great, she said,
    He still may stoop and save me!

And if it be but fate, she said,
    These eyes and red lips, gave me?
What use is left in praying, then? she said.

But if we had our way, she said,
    With men, – then we would love them,
Not as for everyday, she said,
    But with God's stars above them,
And flowers below, to dress the day! she said.

Then hardest hearted men, she said,
    Would only love for kindness;
And all sad women then, she said,
    Should end their tears and blindness:
And Christ save Mari Magdalen! she said.

ERNEST RHYS
Welsh Ballads (1898)

THE LITTLE DANCERS

Lonely, save for a few faint stars, the sky
Dreams; and lonely, below, the little street
Into its gloom retires, secluded and shy.
Scarcely the dumb roar enters this soft retreat;
And all is dark, save where come flooding rays
From a tavern window: there, to the brisk measure
Of an organ that down in an alley merrily plays,
Two children, all alone and no one by,
Holding their tattered frocks, through an airy maze
Of motion, lightly threaded with nimble feet,
Dance sedately: face to face they gaze,
Their eyes shining, grave with a perfect pleasure.

LAURENCE BINYON
London Visions (1896)

DÉCOR DE THÉÂTRE

4

LA MÉLINITE: MOULIN ROUGE

Olivier Metra's Waltz of Roses
   Sheds in a rhythmic shower
   The very petals of the flower;
And all is roses,
   The rouge of petals in a shower.

Down the long hall the dance returning
   Rounds the full circle, rounds
   The perfect rose of lights and sounds,
The rose returning
   Into the circle of its rounds.

Alone, apart, one dancer watches
   Her mirrored, morbid grace;
   Before the mirror, face to face,
Alone she watches
   Her morbid, vague, ambiguous grace.

Before the mirror's dance of shadows
   She dances in a dream,
   And she and they together seem
A dance of shadows;
   Alike the shadows of a dream.

The orange-rosy lamps are trembling
   Between the robes that turn;
   In ruddy flowers of flame that burn
The lights are trembling:
   The shadows and the dancers turn.

And, enigmatically smiling,
    In the mysterious night,
    She dances for her own delight,
A shadow smiling
    Back to a shadow in the night.

ARTHUR SYMONS
London Nights (2nd edition 1897)

SELENE EDEN

My dearest lovers know me not;
    I hide my life and soul from sight;
I conquer all whose blood is hot;
    My mystery is my mail of might.

I had a troupe who danced with me:
    I veiled myself from head to foot;
My girls were nude as they dared be;
    They sang a chorus, I was mute.

But now I fill the widest stage
    Alone, unveiled, without a song;
And still with mystery I engage
    The aching senses of the throng.

A dark-blue vest with stars of gold,
    My only diamond in my hair,
An Indian scarf about me rolled:
    That is the dress I always wear.

And first the sensuous music whets
    The lustful crowd; the dim-lit room
Recalls delights, recalls regrets;
    And then I enter in the gloom.

I glide, I trip, I run, I spin,
    Lapped in the lime-light's aureole.
Hushed are the voices, hushed the din,
    I see men's eyes like glowing coal.

My loosened scarf in odours drenched
    Showers keener hints of sensual bliss;
The music swoons, the light is quenched,
    Into the dark I blow a kiss.

Then, like a long wave rolling home,
    The music gathers speed and sound;
I, dancing, am the music's foam,
    And wilder, fleeter, higher bound,

And fling my feet above my head;
    The light grows, none aside may glance;
Crimson and amber, green and red,
    In blinding baths of these I dance.

And soft, and sweet, and calm, my face
    Looks pure as unsunned chastity,
Even in the whirling triple pace:
    That is my conquering mystery.

JOHN DAVIDSON
In a Music-Hall (1891)

TO ONE IN BEDLAM

With delicate, mad hands, behind his sordid bars,
Surely he hath his posies, which they tear and twine;
Those scentless wisps of straw, that miserably line
His strait, caged universe, whereat the dull world stares,

Pedant and pitiful. O, how his rapt gaze wars
With their stupidity! Know they what dreams divine
Lift his long, laughing reveries like enchaunted wine,
And make his melancholy germane to the stars'?

O lamentable brother! if those pity thee,
Am I not fain of all thy lone eyes promise me;
Half a fool's kingdom, far from men who sow and reap,
All their days, vanity? Better than mortal flowers,
Thy moon-kissed roses seem: better than love or sleep,
The star-crowned solitude of thine oblivious hours!

ERNEST DOWSON
Verses (1896)

WAITING

Within unfriendly walls
    We starve – or starve by stealth.
Oxen fatten in their stalls;
    You guard the harrier's health:
They never can be criminals,
    And can't compete for wealth.
        From the mansion and the palace
            Is there any help or hail
        For the tenants of the alleys,
            Of the workhouse and the jail?

Though lands await our toil,
    And earth half-empty rolls,
Cumberers of English soil,
    We cringe for orts and doles –
Prosperity's accustomed foil,
    Millions of useless souls.

In the gutters and the ditches
    Human vermin festering lurk –
We, the rust upon your riches;
    We, the flaw in all your work.

Come down from where you sit;
    We look to you for aid.
Take us from the miry pit,
    And lead us undismayed:
Say, 'Even you, outcast, unfit,
    Forward with sword and spade!'
       And myriads of us idle
          Would thank you through our tears,
        Though you drove us with a bridle,
          And a whip about our ears!

From cloudy cape to cape
    The teeming waters seethe;
Golden grain and purple grape
    The regions overwreathe.
Will no one help us to escape?
    We scarce have room to breathe.
       You might try to understand us:
          We are waiting night and day
        For a captain to command us,
          And the word we must obey.

JOHN DAVIDSON
The Last Ballad (1899)

4. The Hound of Heaven

THE HOUND OF HEAVEN

BARBEY D'AUREVILLY wrote in 1884 in a review of *À Rebours* that 'after such a book, there is nothing left for the author but to choose between the muzzle of a pistol and the foot of the cross'. Huysmans wrote in 1903 that the choice was made, having become a devout Roman Catholic. Many of the poets of the 'nineties, concerned with problems similar to those which faced the author and the hero of 'the breviary of the Decadence' as Symons called *À Rebours*, found themselves faced with a similar dilemma. Their choice was commonly the same as Huysmans'. 'Some turned Catholic,' wrote Yeats in *The Oxford Book of Modern Verse*, '... that too was a tradition.' Beardsley, Lord Alfred Douglas, Dowson, Johnson, both the ladies who signed themselves 'Michael Field', and Oscar Wilde, became Catholics; Francis Thompson, who had been brought up in a Catholic family, had been intended for the priesthood, and his religious inclinations never left him; John Gray, a Catholic convert, became a priest; in fact rumour had it that 'during the 'nineties there had been so many scandals over so-called "decadents" becoming converts to Catholicism that the Pope had decreed that John Gray, on receiving holy orders, must not remain in England!'[1]

What d'Aurevilly had so acutely analysed in des Esseintes and his creator was not only their disgust with the world and its aims but also the inability of art to answer the problems of existence, and their consequent turning to religion for the answers. An equally perceptive critic might have found the same need in the writers of the 'nineties.

1. *Two Friends*, ed. Fr. Brocard Sewell, London, 1963.

Shaw did write, in the first number of *The Savoy* (January, 1896), that society needed 'refreshment and recreation' and, though he perhaps meant it a little differently from the ordinary man, added that 'in the church alone can our need be truly met'. Yeats points out that 'there are "stars" in poem after poem of certain writers of the 'nineties as though to symbolize an aspiration towards what is inviolate and fixed'.[2] The fixedness of religion, of Catholicism in particular, was attractive, as was the ritual; 'Life must be a ritual' was a phrase of Johnson's that stuck in Yeats's mind. And though the superficial and decorative aspects were no doubt suited to their taste, their religion was by no means insincere. Perhaps the most unconventional in religious matters were Symons, the son of a Methodist minister, and Davidson, the son of a minister in the Evangelical Union.

There were accusations of insincerity. Le Gallienne, who later conducted a long correspondence in the *Daily Chronicle* on the subject 'Is Christianity played out?' and published it as *The Religion of a Literary Man* (1893), complained of the Decadent who 'used his soul /As bitters to the over dulcet sins'. Certainly the refusal to be moral in the Victorian sense and the tendency to make art a religion left poets open to complaint; but many are fairly conventional in their religion, much more so than Yeats, whose mystical visions foreshadow his later and more completely worked-out beliefs. The religious synthesis was as necessary for these poets as it had been for Tennyson and Browning and as it was to be for Eliot.

2. *The Oxford Book of Modern Verse.*

BENEDICTIO DOMINI

Without, the sullen noises of the street!
   The voice of London, inarticulate,
Hoarse and blaspheming, surges in to meet
   The silent blessing of the Immaculate.

Dark is the church, and dim the worshippers,
   Hushed with bowed heads as though by some old spell,
While through the incense-laden air there stirs
   The admonition of a silver bell.

Dark is the church, save where the altar stands,
   Dressed like a bride, illustrious with light,
Where one old priest exalts with tremulous hands
   The one true solace of man's fallen plight.

Strange silence here: without, the sounding street
   Heralds the world's swift passage to the fire:
O Benediction, perfect and complete!
   When shall men cease to suffer and desire?

ERNEST DOWSON
Verses (1896)

MAGIC

2

They wrong with ignorance a royal choice,
Who cavil at my loneliness and labour:
For them, the luring wonder of a voice,
The viol's cry for them, the harp and tabour:
    For me divine austerity,
    And voices of philosophy.

Ah! light imaginations, that discern
No passion in the citadel of passion:
Their fancies lie on flowers; but my thoughts turn
To thoughts and things of an eternal fashion:
    The majesty and dignity
    Of everlasting verity.

Mine is the sultry sunset, when the skies
Tremble with strange, intolerable thunder:
And at the dead of an hushed night, these eyes
Draw down the soaring oracles winged with wonder:
    From the four winds they come to me,
    The Angels of Eternity.

Men pity me; poor men, who pity me!
Poor, charitable, scornful souls of pity!
I choose laborious loneliness: and ye
Lead Love in triumph through the dancing city:
    While death and darkness girdle me,
    I grope for immortality.

LIONEL JOHNSON
Ireland, with Other Poems (1897)

THE HOUND OF HEAVEN

I fled Him, down the nights and down the days;
   I fled Him, down the arches of the years;
I fled Him, down the labyrinthine ways
   Of my own mind; and in the mist of tears
I hid from Him, and under running laughter.
       Up vistaed hopes I sped;
       And shot, precipitated
Adown Titanic glooms of chasmed fears,
   From those strong Feet that followed, followed after.
      But with unhurrying chase,
      And unperturbèd pace,
    Deliberate speed, majestic instancy,
      They beat – and a Voice beat
      More instant than the Feet –
'All things betray thee, who betrayest Me.'

      I pleaded, outlaw-wise,
By many a hearted casement, curtained red,
   Trellised with intertwining charities;
(For, though I knew His love Who followèd,
      Yet was I sore adread
Lest, having Him, I must have naught beside)
But, if one little casement parted wide,
   The gust of His approach would clash it to.
   Fear wist not to evade, as Love wist to pursue.
Across the margent of the world I fled,
   And troubled the gold gateways of the stars,
   Smiting for shelter on their changèd bars;
      Fretted to dulcet jars
And silvern chatter the pale ports o' the moon.
I said to dawn: Be sudden – to eve: Be soon;

With thy young skiey blossoms heap me over
    From this tremendous Lover!
Float thy vague veil about me, lest He see!
  I tempted all His servitors, but to find
My own betrayal in their constancy,
In faith to Him their fickleness to me,
   Their traitorous trueness, and their loyal deceit.
To all swift things for swiftness did I sue;
   Clung to the whistling mane of every wind.
     But whether they swept, smoothly fleet,
     The long savannahs of the blue;
       Or whether, Thunder-driven,
      They clanged his chariot 'thwart a heaven,
Plashy with flying lightnings round the spurn o' their feet:—
  Fear wist not to evade as Love wist to pursue.
      Still with unhurrying chase,
      And unperturbèd pace,
    Deliberate speed, majestic instancy,
      Came on the following Feet,
      And a Voice above their beat –
  'Naught shelters thee, who wilt not shelter Me.'

I sought no more that, after which I strayed,
    In face of man or maid;
But still within the little children's eyes
   Seems something, something that replies,
They at least are for me, surely for me!
I turned me to them very wistfully;
But just as their young eyes grew sudden fair
    With dawning answers there,
Their angel plucked them from me by the hair.
'Come then, ye other children, Nature's – share
With me' (said I) 'your delicate fellowship;
   Let me greet you lip to lip,

Let me twine with you caresses,
    Wantoning
With our Lady-Mother's vagrant tresses,
    Banqueting
With her in her wind-walled palace,
Underneath her azured daïs,
Quaffing, as your taintless way is,
    From a chalice
Lucent-weeping out of the dayspring.'
    So it was done:
I in their delicate fellowship was one —
Drew the bolt of Nature's secrecies.
    I knew all the swift importings
    On the wilful face of skies;
    I knew how the clouds arise
    Spumèd of the wild sea-snortings;
        All that's born or dies
    Rose and drooped with — made them shapers
Of mine own moods, or wailful or divine —
    With them joyed and was bereaven.
    I was heavy with the even,
    When she lit her glimmering tapers
    Round the day's dead sanctities.
    I laughed in the morning's eyes.
I triumphed and I saddened with all weather,
    Heaven and I wept together,
And its sweet tears were salt with mortal mine;
Against the red throb of its sunset-heart
    I laid my own to beat,
    And share commingling heat;
But not by that, by that, was eased my human smart.
In vain my tears were wet on Heaven's grey cheek.
For ah! we know not what each other says,
    These things and I; in sound *I* speak —

Their sound is but their stir, they speak by silences.
Nature, poor stepdame, cannot slake my drouth;
    Let her, if she would owe me,
Drop yon blue bosom-veil of sky, and show me
    The breasts o' her tenderness:
Never did any milk of hers once bless
      My thirsting mouth.
      Nigh and nigh draws the chase,
      With unperturbèd pace
    Deliberate speed, majestic instancy;
      And past those noisèd Feet
      A voice comes yet more fleet —
    'Lo! naught contents thee, who content'st not Me.'

Naked I wait Thy love's uplifted stroke!
My harness piece by piece Thou hast hewn from me,
    And smitten me to my knee;
    I am defenceless utterly.
    I slept, methinks, and woke,
And, slowly gazing, find me stripped in sleep.
In the rash lustihead of my young powers,
    I shook the pillaring hours
And pulled my life upon me; grimed with smears,
I stand amid the dust o' the mounded years —
My mangled youth lies dead beneath the heap.
My days have crackled and gone up in smoke,
Have puffed and burst as sun-starts on a stream.
    Yea, faileth now even dream
The dreamer, and the lute the lutanist;
Even the linked fantasies, in whose blossomy twist
I swung the earth a trinket at my wrist,
Are yielding; cords of all too weak account
For earth with heavy griefs so overplussed.
    Ah! is Thy love indeed

A weed, albeit an amaranthine weed,
Suffering no flowers except its own to mount?
    Ah! must —
    Designer infinite! —
Ah! must Thou char the wood ere Thou canst limn with it?
My freshness spent its wavering shower i' the dust;
And now my heart is as a broken fount,
Wherein tear-drippings stagnate, spilt down ever
    From the dank thoughts that shiver
Upon the sighful branches of my mind.
    Such is; what is to be?
The pulp so bitter, how shall taste the rind?
I dimly guess what Time in mists confounds;
Yet ever and anon a trumpet sounds
From the hid battlements of Eternity,
Those shaken mists a space unsettle, then
Round the half-glimpsèd turrets slowly wash again;
    But not ere him who summoneth
    I first have seen, enwound
With glooming robes purpureal, cypress-crowned;
His name I know, and what his trumpet saith.
Whether man's heart or life it be which yields
    Thee harvest, must Thy harvest fields
    Be dunged with rotten death?
      Now of that long pursuit
      Comes on at hand the bruit;
That Voice is round me like a bursting sea:
      'And is thy earth so marred,
      Shattered in shard on shard?
Lo, all things fly thee, for thou fliest Me!

    'Strange, piteous, futile thing!
Wherefore should any set thee love apart?
Seeing none but I makes much of naught' (He said),

'And human love needs human meriting:
　　　How hast thou merited –
Of all man's clotted clay the dingiest clot?
　　　Alack, thou knowest not
How little worthy of any love thou art!
Whom wilt thou find to love ignoble thee,
　　　Save Me, save only Me?
All which I took from thee I did but take,
　　　Not for thy harms,
But just that thou might'st seek it in My arms.
　　　All which thy child's mistake
Fancies as lost, I have stored for thee at home:
　　　Rise, clasp My hand, and come.'

　　　Halts by me that footfall:
　　　Is my gloom, after all,
Shade of His hand, outstretched caressingly?
　　　'Ah, fondest, blindest, weakest,
　　　I am He Whom thou seekest!
Thou dravest love from thee, who dravest Me.'

FRANCIS THOMPSON
Poems (1893)

'LORD, IF THOU ART NOT PRESENT'

　　Lord, if thou art not present, where shall I
　　Seek thee the absent? If thou art everywhere,
　　How is it that I do not see thee nigh?

　　Thou dwellest in a light remote and fair.
　　How can I reach that light, Lord? I beseech
　　Thee, teach my seeking, and thyself declare

Thyself the sought to me. Unless thou teach
Me, Lord, I cannot seek; nor can I find
Thee, if thou wilt not come within my reach.

Lord, let me seek, with sturdy heart and mind,
In passion of desire and longingly.
Let me desire thee, seeking thee; and find . . .

Loving thee, find thee; love thee, finding thee.

JOHN GRAY
Spiritual Poems (1896)

THE SILENT HEAVENS

Here I wander about, and here I mournfully ponder:
    Weary to me is the sun, weary the coming of night:
Here is captivity still, there would be captivity yonder:
    Like to myself are the rest, smitten is all with a blight.

Much I complain of my state to my own heart heavily
    beating:
        Much to the stars I complain: much to the universe
            cold;
The stars that of old were fixed, in spheres their courses
    repeating;
        Solidly once were they fixed, and with them their
            spheres were rolled.

Then through the space of the spheres to the steadfast
    empyrean
        Echo on echo to Earth answered her manifold cries:
Earth was the centre of things, and the threne of all, or the
    pæan,
        Bearing hell in her heart, on her bosom all life that
            dies.

If they were fixed, as of old, in their firmament solid and
   vaulted,
      Then might the echo of woe or of laughter
        reverberate thence:
Nor my voice alone, but to them all voices exalted,
    Should with due answer be met, murmuring sweet to
     the sense.

But they roll on their way through the void, the inane
   unretentive:
     Past them all voices stream into the echoless space.
Where is the pitying grace, that once was prayer's
   incentive,
     Where is the ear that heard, and the face that once
      answered to face?

R. W. DIXON
The Last Poems of Richard Watson Dixon, D.D. (1905)

VENI CREATOR

So humble things Thou hast borne for us, O God,
Left'st Thou a path of lowliness untrod?
Yes, one, till now; another Olive-Garden.
For we endure the tender pain of pardon, –
One with another we forbear. Give heed,
Look at the mournful world Thou hast decreed.
The time has come. At last we hapless men
Know all our haplessness all through. Come, then,
Endure undreamed humility: Lord of Heaven,
Come to our ignorant hearts and be forgiven.

ALICE MEYNELL
Poems (1898)

Lionel Johnson

THE DARK ANGEL

Dark Angel, with thine aching lust
To rid the world of penitence:
Malicious Angel, who still dost
My soul such subtile violence!

Because of thee, no thought, no thing,
Abides for me undesecrate:
Dark Angel, ever on the wing,
Who never reachest me too late!

When music sounds, then changest thou
Its silvery to a sultry fire:
Nor will thine envious heart allow
Delight untortured by desire.

Through thee, the gracious Muses turn
To Furies, O mine Enemy!
And all the things of beauty burn
With flames of evil ecstasy.

Because of thee, the land of dreams
Becomes a gathering place of fears:
Until tormented slumber seems
One vehemence of useless tears.

When sunlight glows upon the flowers,
Or ripples down the dancing sea:
Thou, with thy troop of passionate powers,
Beleaguerest, bewilderest, me.

Within the breath of autumn woods,
Within the winter silences:
Thy venomous spirit stirs and broods,
O Master of impieties!

The ardour of red flame is thine,
And thine the steely soul of ice:
Thou poisonest the fair design
Of nature, with unfair device.

Apples of ashes, golden bright;
Waters of bitterness, how sweet!
O banquet of a foul delight,
Prepared by thee, dark Paraclete!

Thou art the whisper in the gloom,
The hinting tone, the haunting laugh:
Thou art the adorner of my tomb,
The minstrel of mine epitaph.

I fight thee, in the Holy Name!
Yet, what thou dost, is what God saith:
Tempter! should I escape thy flame,
Thou wilt have helped my soul from Death:

The second Death, that never dies,
That cannot die, when time is dead:
Live Death, wherein the lost soul cries,
Eternally uncomforted.

Dark Angel, with thine aching lust!
Of two defeats, of two despairs:
Less dread, a change to drifting dust,
Than thine eternity of cares.

Do what thou wilt, thou shalt not so,
Dark Angel! triumph over me:
Lonely, unto the Lone I go;
Divine, to the Divinity.

LIONEL JOHNSON
Poems (1895)

INSOMNIA

He wakened quivering on a golden rack
    Inlaid with gems: no sign of change, no fear
    Or hope of death came near;
Only the empty ether hovered black
    About him stretched upon his living bier,
Of old by Marlin's Master deftly wrought:
    Two Seraphim of Gabriel's helpful race
    In that far nook of space
With iron levers wrenched and held him taut.

The Seraph at his head was Agony;
    Delight, more terrible, stood at his feet:
    Their sixfold pinions beat
The darkness, or were spread immovably,
    Poising the rack, whose jewelled fabric meet
To strain a god, did fitfully unmask
    With olive light of chrysoprases dim
    The smiling Seraphim
Implacably intent upon their task.

JOHN DAVIDSON
The Last Ballad (1899)

THE VEIL OF LIGHT

Here, where the vague winds, tired, come to sleep,
Here, where they hide when hunted by the rain;
From this point whence the world looks far and deep,
We gaze triumphant on the earth's dull plain.

How hardly won! – but now this comely peace:
Even the sea-tang in the mellow air
Breathes harshly, and its strength disturbs the ease
Of yon thin cloud soft falling from God's Hair.

Ah, that bright cloud! – a curtain from the sky;
That shifting filmy thing, that drifting gauze:
The dooms that 'neath its trembling shadows lie,
Though suns be in our hearts, must give us pause.

All down the valleys of the universe,
Through firmaments to where the tall stars end,
The terror lurks, and stabs us like a curse,
Whom Fear binds close together, O my friend!

Blank dreams are there that make a mock of life;
And all of sinister that round the bed
Crawl in dark hours, alive and wet with strife;
And all the thoughts when no more words are said.

And what unknown is there to mar our way?
What more, O Blessèd Lord! what vile thing more
Lies hid behind that mass of whitened grey?
What furtive venom is there still in store?

Hear, in Thy lofty place, Thy children calling!
Dead leaves, we ride upon the wings of night:
Remove, Lord God most High, this shroud appalling —
This hard, intolerable Veil of Light!

VINCENT O'SULLIVAN
Poems (1896)

A SHROPSHIRE LAD

43

THE IMMORTAL PART

When I meet the morning beam,
Or lay me down at night to dream,
I hear my bones within me say,
'Another night, another day.

'When shall this slough of sense be cast,
This dust of thoughts be laid at last,
The man of flesh and soul be slain
And the man of bone remain?

'This tongue that talks, these lungs that shout,
These thews that hustle us about,
This brain that fills the skull with schemes,
And its humming hive of dreams, —

'These to-day are proud in power
And lord it in their little hour:
The immortal bones obey control
Of dying flesh and dying soul.

''Tis long till eve and morn are gone:
Slow the endless night comes on,
And late to fulness grows the birth
That shall last as long as earth.

'Wanderers eastward, wanderers west,
Know you why you cannot rest?
'Tis that every mother's son
Travails with a skeleton.

'Lie down in the bed of dust;
Bear the fruit that bear you must;
Bring the eternal seed to light,
And morn is all the same as night.

'Rest you so from trouble sore,
Fear the heat o' the sun no more,
Nor the snowing winter wild,
Now you labour not with child.

'Empty vessel, garment cast,
We that wore you long shall last.
– Another night, another day.'
So my bones within me say.

Therefore they shall do my will
To-day while I am master still,
And flesh and soul, now both are strong,
Shall hale the sullen slaves along,

Before this fire of sense decay,
This smoke of thought blow clean away,
And leave with ancient night alone
The stedfast and enduring bone.

A. E. HOUSMAN
A Shropshire Lad (1896)

QUISQUE SUOS MANES

What have you seen, eyes of strange fire! What have you
    seen,
Far off, how far away! long since, so long ago!
To fill you with this jewel flame, this frozen glow:
Haunted and hard, still eyes, malignant and serene?
In what wild place of fear, what Pan's wood, have you been,
That struck your lustrous rays into a burning snow?
What agonies were yours? What never equalled woe?
Eyes of strange fire, strange eyes of fire! on what dread scene?

Smitten and purged, you saw the red deeps of your sin:
You saw there death in life; you will see life in death.
The sunlight shrank away, the moon came wan and thin,
Among the summer trees the sweet winds held their breath.
Now those celestial lights, which you can never win,
Haunt you, and pierce, and blind. The Will of God so saith.

LIONEL JOHNSON
Ireland, with Other Poems (1897)

THE SECRET ROSE

Far off, most secret, and inviolate Rose,
Enfold me in my hour of hours; where those
Who sought thee in the Holy Sepulchre,
Or in the wine vat, dwell beyond the stir
And tumult of defeated dreams; and deep
Among pale eyelids, heavy with the sleep
Men have named beauty. Thy great leaves enfold
The ancient beards, the helms of ruby and gold

Of the crowned Magi; and the king whose eyes
Saw the Pierced Hands and Rood of elder rise
In druid vapour and make the torches dim;
Till vain frenzy awoke and he died; and him
Who met Fand walking among flaming dew
By a grey shore where the wind never blew,
And lost the world and Emer for a kiss;
And him who drove the gods out of their liss,
And till a hundred morns had flowered red,
Feasted and wept the barrows of his dead;
And the proud dreaming king who flung the crown
And sorrow away, and calling bard and clown
Dwelt among wine-stained wanderers in deep woods;
And him who sold tillage, and house, and goods,
And sought through lands and islands numberless years,
Until he found with laughter and with tears,
A woman, of so shining loveliness,
That men threshed corn at midnight by a tress,
A little stolen tress. I, too, await
The hour of thy great wind of love and hate.
When shall the stars be blown about the sky,
Like the sparks blown out of a smithy, and die?
Surely thine hour has come, thy great wind blows,
Far off, most secret, and inviolate Rose?

W. B. YEATS
The Wind Among the Reeds (1899)

NUNS OF THE PERPETUAL ADORATION

Calm, sad, secure; behind high convent walls,
    These watch the sacred lamp, these watch and pray:
And it is one with them when evening falls,
    And one with them the cold return of day.

These heed not time; their nights and days they make
    Into a long, returning rosary,
Whereon their lives are threaded for Christ's sake:
    Meekness and vigilance and chastity.

A vowed patrol, in silent companies,
    Life-long they keep before the living Christ:
In the dim church, their prayers and penances
    Are fragrant incense to the Sacrificed.

Outside, the world is wild and passionate;
    Man's weary laughter and his sick despair
Entreat at their impenetrable gate:
    They heed no voices in their dream of prayer.

They saw the glory of the world displayed;
    They saw the bitter of it, and the sweet;
They knew the roses of the world should fade,
    And be trod under by the hurrying feet.

Therefore they rather put away desire,
    And crossed their hands and came to sanctuary;
And veiled their heads and put on coarse attire:
    Because their comeliness was vanity.

And there they rest; they have serene insight
    Of the illuminating dawn to be:
Mary's sweet Star dispels for them the night,
    The proper darkness of humanity.

Calm, sad, secure; with faces worn and mild:
    Surely their choice of vigil is the best?
Yea! for our roses fade, the world is wild;
    But there, beside the altar, there, is rest.

ERNEST DOWSON
Verses (1896)

GOOD FRIDAY

He hangs a dead corpse on the tree,
    Who made the whole world's life to spring:
    And, as some outcast, shameful, thing
The Lord of all we see.

Darkness falls thick to shroud the time:
    Nature herself breaks up, and cries:
    Even from the grave shocked ghosts arise,
At this tremendous crime.

Speak not: no human voice may tell
    The secrets, which these hours enfold:
    By treacherous hands to traitors sold,
God yields Himself to Hell.

Speak not, draw close: through stricken heart
    Drink in the sense of all that's here:
    The shame, the cross, the nails, the spear,
Rending His soul apart.

Ah! and far crueller, far, than they,
    (Tools, and mere symbols these) our sin!
    Breathe to thyself, soul, deep within,
''Twas I, that caused this day.'

Speak not: He speaks not: no reproach
    Falls from Those dying lips on thee:
    No vengeance, muttering ills to be,
Bars thy devout approach.

Stricken, unmurmuring, dead, divine,
   This day He hangs, as He hung of old:
    Only the dire sight cries, 'Behold!
Was ever love like Mine?'

SELWYN IMAGE
Poems and Carols (1894)

A CAROL FOR CHRISTMAS EVE

We are but of such mortal mould,
   Nos exaudi, Domine!
That the night can scarce withhold
   In its shroud our sins from Thee.

That night comes, when Thou shalt come
   Nos exaudi, Domine!
From Thy home to this sad home,
   And die for us upon the tree.

If then the stars shine out so bright,
   Nos exaudi, Domine!
That Thou seest by their light,
   How great our sins and many be;

Thou wilt come, as they were not,
   Nos exaudi, Domine!
Or as they were all forgot,
   Or forgiven, Lord, by Thee.

HERBERT HORNE
Diversi Colores (1891)

A MEDITATION FOR CHRISTMAS

Consider, O my soul, what morn is this!
    Whereon the eternal Lord of all things made,
For us, poor mortals, and our endless bliss,
    Came down from heaven; and, in a manger laid,
    The first, rich, offerings of our ransom paid:
Consider, O my soul, what morn is this!

Consider what estate of fearful woe
    Had then been ours, had He refused this birth;
From sin to sin tossed vainly to and fro,
    Hell's playthings, o'er a doomed and helpless earth!
    Had He from us withheld His priceless worth,
Consider man's estate of fearful woe!

Consider to what joys He bids thee rise,
    Who comes, Himself, life's bitter cup to drain!
Ah! look on this sweet Child, Whose innocent eyes,
    Ere all be done, shall close in mortal pain,
    That thou at last Love's Kingdom may'st attain:
Consider to what joys He bids thee rise!

Consider all this wonder, O my soul:
    And in thine inmost shrine make music sweet!
Yea, let the world, from furthest pole to pole,
    Join in thy praises this dread birth to greet;
    Kneeling to kiss thy Saviour's infant feet!
Consider all this wonder, O my soul!

SELWYN IMAGE
Poems and Carols (1894)

THE CHURCH OF A DREAM

Sadly the dead leaves rustle in the whistling wind,
Around the weather-worn, gray church, low down the
   vale:
The Saints in golden vesture shake before the gale;
The glorious windows shake, where still they dwell
   enshrined;
Old Saints, by long dead, shrivelled hands, long since
   designed:
There still, although the world autumnal be, and pale,
Still in their golden vesture the old saints prevail;
Alone with Christ, desolate else, left by mankind.

Only one ancient Priest offers the Sacrifice,
Murmuring holy Latin immemorial:
Swaying with tremulous hands the old censer full of spice,
In gray, sweet incense clouds; blue, sweet clouds mystical:
To him, in place of men, for he is old, suffice
Melancholy remembrances and vesperal.

LIONEL JOHNSON
Poems (1895)

TO THE ROSE UPON THE ROOD OF TIME

Red Rose, proud Rose, sad Rose of all my days!
Come near me, while I sing the ancient ways:
Cuhoollin battling with the bitter tide;
The Druid, gray, wood-nurtured, quiet-eyed,
Who cast round Fergus dreams, and ruin untold;
And thine own sadness, whereof stars, grown old

In dancing silver sandalled on the sea,
Sing in their high and lonely melody.
Come near, that no more blinded by man's fate,
I find under the boughs of love and hate,
In all poor foolish things that live a day,
Eternal Beauty wandering on her way.

Come near, come near, come near – Ah, leave me still
A little space for the rose-breath to fill!
Lest I no more hear common things that crave;
The weak worm hiding down in its small cave,
The field mouse running by me in the grass,
And heavy mortal hopes that toil and pass;
But seek alone to hear the strange things said
By God to the bright hearts of those long dead,
And learn to chaunt a tongue men do not know.
Come near; I would, before my time to go,
Sing of old Eire and the ancient ways:
Red Rose, proud Rose, sad Rose of all my days.

W. B. YEATS
Poems (1899)

ENTHUSIASTS

Let your swords flash, and wound the golden air of God:
Bright steel, to meet and cleave the splendour of His sun!
Now is a war of wars in majesty begun:
Red shall the cornfields ripen, where our horses trod,
Where scythe nor sickle swept, but smote war's iron rod:
Where the stars rose and set, and saw the blood still run.
So shall men tell of us, and dread our deeds, though done:
New annals yet shall praise time's fiercest period.

Let your swords flash, and wound the glowing air : now play
A glorious dance of death, with clash and gleam of sword.
Did Syrian sun and moon stand still on Israel's day?
Those orbs halt over Ajalon at Joshua's word?
Of us, who ride for God, shall Christian children say:
To battle, see! flash by armed angels of the Lord.

LIONEL JOHNSON
Poems (1895)

THE VALLEY OF THE BLACK PIG

The dews drop slowly and dreams gather : unknown spears
Suddenly hurtle before my dream-awakened eyes,
And then the clash of fallen horsemen and the cries
Of unknown perishing armies beat about my ears.
We who still labour by the cromlec on the shore,
The grey cairn on the hill, when day sinks drowned in dew,
Being weary of the world's empires, bow down to you
Master of the still stars and of the flaming door.

W. B. YEATS
The Wind Among the Reeds (1899)

EXTREME UNCTION

Upon the eyes, the lips, the feet,
  On all the passages of sense,
The atoning oil is spread with sweet
  Renewal of lost innocence.

The feet, that lately ran so fast
  To meet desire, are soothly sealed;
The eyes, that were so often cast
  On vanity, are touched and healed.

From troublous sights and sounds set free;
   In such a twilight hour of breath,
Shall one retrace his life, or see,
    Through shadows, the true face of death?

Vials of mercy! Sacring oils!
   I know not where nor when I come,
Nor through what wanderings and toils,
    To crave of you Viaticum.

Yet, when the walls of flesh grow weak,
   In such an hour, it well may be,
Through mist and darkness, light will break,
    And each anointed sense will see.

ERNEST DOWSON
Verses (1896)

EPILOGUE: CREDO

Each, in himself, his hour to be and cease
   Endures alone, but who of men shall dare,
   Sole with himself, his single burden bear,
All the long day until the night's release?

Yet, ere night falls, and the last shadows close,
   This labour of himself is each man's lot;
   All he has gained of earth shall be forgot,
Himself he leaves behind him when he goes.

If he has any valiancy within,
   If he has made his life his very own,
   If he has loved or laboured, and has known
A strenuous virtue, or a strenuous sin;

Then, being dead, his life was not all vain,
   For he has saved what most desire to lose,
   And he has chosen what the few must choose,
Since life, once lived, shall not return again.

For of our time we lose so large a part
   In serious trifles, and so oft let slip
   The wine of every moment, at the lip
Its moment, and the moment of the heart.

We are awake so little on the earth,
   And we shall sleep so long, and rise so late,
   If there is any knocking at that gate
Which is the gate of death, the gate of birth.

ARTHUR SYMONS
London Nights (2nd edition 1897)

5. *Love and Death*

LOVE AND DEATH

THERE is no evidence that poets of the 'nineties loved or died more frequently than those of any other period. There was certainly nothing new in the traditional poetic subjects of love and death, and many of the poems are of the period because of their style rather than their content.

Nonetheless, some poets sang of loves quite distinct from traditional types. Le Gallienne, reviewing John Gray's *Silverpoints* (1893), greets Gray's line 'What bonny hair our child will have' with the comment 'Is not this absurdly domestic in a decadent? Really Mr Gray must check these natural impulses.' Certainly bought love, casual love, and the 'love that dare not speak its name' (though it seems to have written it) were being claimed as subject matter for poetry. It had been done before, even in the Victorian period; Rossetti had written of

> Lazy laughing languid Jenny,
> Fond of a kiss and fond of a guinea;

Swinburne's poems had hymned a variety of loves, and Wilde had described 'The Harlot's House'. But Dowson could still feel nervous about his 'Cynara': 'I have just seen the proofs of my "Cynara" poem for the April Hobby. It looks less indecent in print, but I am still nervous! though I admire Horne's audacity.'[1]

The insistence on the more perverse type of subject was a combination of a striving for freedom in choice of subject matter, a desire to shock, and a love of the artificial or

1. *The Letters of Ernest Dowson*, ed. Desmond Flower and Henry Maas, 1967.

unnatural. It was also a reaction against the hypocrisy of the Victorian pretence of rectitude, the true superficiality of which has been demonstrated by Steven Marcus's *The Other Victorians*. But freedom of subject matter often meant concentration on the perverse or erotic, a fact recognized by parodists. Symons, in the person of Arthur in Owen Seaman's 'A Vigo-Street Eclogue', admits his propensities:

> What's Nature's law compared with women's?
>
> JOHN
>
> For this enigma go to S-m-ns;
> He is the –
>
> ARTHUR
>   Yes, I am, I know,
> The devil of a Romeo!

And Lionel Johnson, in the following parody from his short story 'Incurable' (from *The Pageant* of 1896) catches the more extreme of the lyrics of Symons or Wratislaw (like the latter's 'The Conquest of Sense').

> Sometimes, in very joy of shame,
> Our flesh becomes one living flame:
> And she and I
> Are no more separate, but the same.
>
> Ardour and agony unite;
> Desire, delirium, delight:
> And I and she
> Faint in the fierce and fevered night.
>
> Her body music is: and ah,
> The accords of lute and viola,
> When she and I
> Play on live limbs love's opera!

Nowhere is there the same extreme in poems that deal with death. Plarr's witty and urbane epitaph rejects ponderous tombstone triteness, but he does not shock. Though death confirms and symbolizes the tragedy that colours the 'nineties, the subject which occurs more frequently is not death but decline, for which see the final section.

A QUESTION AND AN ANSWER

The Question: What is Love? Is Love in this,
That flies between us, in a kiss?
Nay, what is Love? Is Love the zest,
That wakes, when I unloose my breast?
But what is Love? Say now: who knows,
Or where he lurks, or how he shows?

The Answer: Dearest, Truth is stern, I fear:
Love, as yet, can scarce be here.

Love is poor; nay, Love is sorry;
  Tears, not kisses, chiefly stay him:
His sad weeds best tell his story;
  Vain delights befool, bewray him.

Truth, alas! is hard to bear:
Know, as yet, Love is not here.

But, when the evil days are come,
  If those same lips, which kiss you now,
Still make your tearful eyes their home,
  And chide the sorrow from your brow;

Then say to your own heart, my Dear:
Abide, poor heart, for Love is here.

Love is a light, in darkened ways;
  Love is a path, in pathless lands;
Love is a fire, in winter days;
  A staff, in chill, unsteady hands.

Speak to your heart, my own, my Dear;
Say: this is Love, and Love is here.

HERBERT HORNE
Diversi Colores (1891)

NERVES

The modern malady of love is nerves.
Love, once a simple madness, now observes
The stages of his passionate disease,
And is twice sorrowful because he sees,
Inch by inch entering, the fatal knife.
O health of simple minds, give me your life,
And let me, for one midnight, cease to hear
The clock for ever ticking in my ear,
The clock that tells the minutes in my brain.
It is not love, nor love's despair, this pain
That shoots a witless, keener pang across
The simple agony of love and loss.
Nerves, nerves! O folly of a child who dreams
Of heaven, and, waking in the darkness, screams.

ARTHUR SYMONS
Dated by Symons 1897
Reprinted in *Collected Works* (1924)

WHITE HELIOTROPE

The feverish room and that white bed,
    The tumbled skirts upon a chair,
    The novel flung half-open, where
Hat, hair-pins, puffs, and paints, are spread;

The mirror that has sucked your face
    Into its secret deep of deeps,
    And there mysteriously keeps
Forgotten memories of grace;

And you, half dressed and half awake,
    Your slant eyes strangely watching me,
    And I, who watch you drowsily,
With eyes that, having slept not, ache;

This (need one dread? nay, dare one hope?)
    Will rise, a ghost of memory, if
    Ever again my handkerchief
Is scented with White Heliotrope.

ARTHUR SYMONS
London Nights (2nd edition 1897)

SPRING-SONG

Ah love, the sweet spring blossoms cling
To many a broken wind-tossed bough,
And young birds among branches sing
That mutely hung till now.

The little new-born things which lie
In dewy meadows, sleep and dream
Beside the brook that twinkles by
To some great lonely stream.

And children, now the day is told,
From many a warm and cosy nest,
Look up to see the young moon hold
The old moon to her breast.

Dear love, my pulses throb and start
To-night with longings sweet and new,
And young hopes beat within a heart
Grown old in loving you.

DOLLIE RADFORD
A Light Load (1891)

A SHROPSHIRE LAD

13

When I was one-and-twenty
   I heard a wise man say,
'Give crowns and pounds and guineas
   But not your heart away;
Give pearls away and rubies
   But keep your fancy free.'
But I was one-and-twenty,
   No use to talk to me.

When I was one-and-twenty
   I heard him say again,
'The heart out of the bosom
   Was never given in vain;
'Tis paid with sighs a plenty
   And sold for endless rue.'
And I am two-and-twenty,
   And oh, 'tis true, 'tis true.

A. E. HOUSMAN
A Shropshire Lad (1896)

DOWN BY THE SALLEY GARDENS

Down by the salley gardens my love and I did meet;
She passed the salley gardens with little snow-white feet.
She bid me take love easy, as the leaves grow on the tree;
But I, being young and foolish, with her would not agree.

In a field by the river my love and I did stand,
And on my leaning shoulder she laid her snow-white hand.
She bid me take life easy, as the grass grows on the weirs;
But I was young and foolish, and now am full of tears.

W. B. YEATS
Poems (1899)

PLYMOUTH HARBOUR

A SONG

Oh, what know they of harbours
 Who toss not on the sea!
They tell of fairer havens,
 But none so fair there be

As Plymouth town outstretching
 Her quiet arms to me;
Her breast's broad welcome spreading
 From Mewstone to Penlee.

Ah, with this home-thought, darling,
 Come crowding thoughts of thee.
Oh, what know they of harbours
 Who toss not on the sea!

ERNEST RADFORD
Old and New (1895)

SAINT GERMAIN-EN-LAYE
(1887–1895)

Through the green boughs I hardly saw thy face,
They twined so close: the sun was in mine eyes;
And now the sullen trees in sombre lace
Stand bare beneath the sinister, sad skies.

O sun and summer! Say in what far night,
The gold and green, the glory of thine head,
Of bough and branch have fallen? Oh, the white
Gaunt ghosts that flutter where thy feet have sped,

Across the terrace that is desolate,
And rang then with thy laughter, ghost of thee,
That holds its shroud up with most delicate,
Dead fingers, and behind the ghost of me,

Tripping fantastic with a mouth that jeers
At roseal flowers of youth the turbid streams
Toss in derision down the barren years
To death the host of all our golden dreams.

ERNEST DOWSON
Decorations (1899)

AEDH WISHES FOR THE CLOTHS
OF HEAVEN

Had I the heavens' embroidered cloths,
Enwrought with golden and silver light,
The blue and the dim and the dark cloths
Of night and light and the half light,

I would spread the cloths under your feet:
But I, being poor, have only my dreams;
I have spread my dreams under your feet;
Tread softly because you tread on my dreams.

W. B. YEATS
The Wind Among the Reeds (1899)

THE TWO TREES

Beloved, gaze in thine own heart,
The holy tree is growing there;
From joy the holy branches start,
And all the trembling flowers they bear.
The changing colours of its fruit
Have dowered the stars with merry light;
The surety of its hidden root
Has planted quiet in the night;
The shaking of its leafy head
Has given the waves their melody,
And made my lips and music wed,
Murmuring a wizard song for thee.
There, through bewildered branches, go
Winged Loves borne on in gentle strife,
Tossing and tossing to and fro
The flaming circle of our life.
When looking on their shaken hair,
And dreaming how they dance and dart,
Thine eyes grow full of tender care:
Beloved, gaze in thine own heart.

Gaze no more in the bitter glass
The demons, with their subtle guile,
Lift up before us when they pass,
Or only gaze a little while;

For there a fatal image grows,
With broken boughs, and blackened leaves,
And roots half hidden under snows
Driven by a storm that ever grieves.
For all things turn to barrenness
In the dim glass the demons hold,
The glass of outer weariness,
Made when God slept in times of old.
There, through the broken branches, go
The ravens of unresting thought;
Peering and flying to and fro,
To see men's souls bartered and bought.
When they are heard upon the wind,
And when they shake their wings; alas!
Thy tender eyes grow all unkind:
Gaze no more in the bitter glass.

W. B. YEATS
Poems (1899)

LES DEMOISELLES DE SAUVE

Beautiful ladies through the orchard pass;
Bend under crutched-up branches, forked and low;
Trailing their samet palls o'er dew-drenched grass.

Pale blossoms, looking on proud Jacqueline,
Blush to the colour of her finger tips,
And rosy knuckles, laced with yellow lace.

High-crested Berthe discerns, with slant, clinched eyes,
Amid the leaves pink faces of the skies;
She locks her plaintive hands Sainte-Margot-wise.

Ysabeau follows last, with languorous pace;
Presses, voluptuous, to her bursting lips,
With backward stoop, a bunch of eglantine.

Courtly ladies through the orchard pass;
Bow low, as in lords' halls; and springtime grass
Tangles a snare to catch the tapering toe.

JOHN GRAY
Silverpoints (1893)

PARADISE WALK

She is living in Paradise Walk,
With the dirt and the noise of the street;
And heaven flies up, if she talk,
With Paradise down at her feet.

She laughs through a summer of curls;
She moves in a garden of grace:
Her glance is a treasure of pearls,
How saved from the deeps of her face!

And the magical reach of her thigh
Is the measure, with which God began
To build up the peace of the sky,
And fashion the pleasures of man.

With Paradise down at her feet,
While heaven flies up if she talk;
With the dirt and the noise of the street,
She is living in Paradise Walk.

HERBERT HORNE
Diversi Colores (1891)

SONG

In the first light of the morning,
    When the thrush sang loud and clear,
And the black-bird hailed day's dawning,
    How I wished my love could hear.

When the sun shone on the sand there,
    And the roses bloomed above,
And the blue waves kissed the land there,
    How I longed to see my love.

Now the birds good-night are calling,
    And the moonbeams come and go,
And my tears are falling, falling,
    Because I want him so.

DOLLIE RADFORD
A Light Load (1891)

A SHROPSHIRE LAD

21

BREDON HILL

In summertime on Bredon
    The bells they sound so clear;
Round both the shires they ring them
    In steeples far and near,
    A happy noise to hear.

Here of a Sunday morning
    My love and I would lie,
And see the coloured counties,
    And hear the larks so high
    About us in the sky.

The bells would ring to call her
   In valleys miles away:
'Come all to church, good people;
   Good people, come and pray.'
   But here my love would stay.

And I would turn and answer
   Among the springing thyme,
'Oh, peal upon our wedding,
   And we will hear the chime,
   And come to church in time.'

But when the snows at Christmas
   On Bredon top were strown,
My love rose up so early
   And stole out unbeknown
   And went to church alone.

They tolled the one bell only,
   Groom there was none to see,
The mourners followed after,
   And so to church went she,
   And would not wait for me.

The bells they sound on Bredon,
   And still the steeples hum,
'Come all to church, good people.' –
   Oh, noisy bells, be dumb;
   I hear you, I will come.

A. E. HOUSMAN
A Shropshire Lad (1896)

'CEASE SMILING, DEAR! A LITTLE WHILE BE SAD'

Dum nos fata sinunt, oculos satiemus Amore
PROPERTIUS

Cease smiling, Dear! a little while be sad,
   Here in the silence, under the wan moon;
Sweet are thine eyes, but how can I be glad,
    Knowing they change so soon?

For Love's sake, Dear, be silent! Cover me
   In the deep darkness of thy falling hair:
Fear is upon me and the memory
    Of what is all men's share.

O could this moment be perpetuate!
   Must we grow old, and leaden-eyed and gray,
And taste no more the wild and passionate
    Love sorrows of to-day?

Grown old, and faded, Sweet! and past desire,
   Let memory die, lest there be too much ruth,
Remembering the old, extinguished fire
    Of our divine, lost youth.

O red pomegranate of thy perfect mouth!
   My lips' life-fruitage, might I taste and die,
Here in thy garden, where the scented south
    Wind chastens agony;

Reap death from thy live lips in one long kiss,
   And look my last into thine eyes and rest:
What sweets had life to me sweeter than this
    Swift dying on thy breast?

Or, if that may not be, for Love's sake, Dear!
   Keep silence still, and dream that we shall lie,
Red mouth to mouth, entwined, and always hear
     The south wind's melody,

Here in thy garden, through the sighing boughs,
   Beyond the reach of time and chance and change,
And bitter life and death, and broken vows,
     That sadden and estrange.

ERNEST DOWSON
Verses (1896)

A SUMMER'S DAY

Overhead a sapphire sky;
   Blossom of the may-trees round:
   On the warm, lush, meadow-ground,
Where the sorrel blooms, we lie.

Psyche-winged, in gold and white,
   Butterflies float past: the earth,
   'Neath the charm of summer's birth,
Thrills with delicate delight.

Softly breathes a southern wind;
   Sings for joy a lark above:
   Oh! what paradise of love
Fairer may our spirits find!

Far away is London town,
   As a world unknown, forgot:
   Misery and sins are not!
Nothing now for tears or frown!

Lean, my Dearest, lean your head
　　Quietly against me. So!
　　Listen, while I whisper low
Words, that hardly may be said.

Nay, your spirit lifts the veil
　　From love, trembling to confess:
　　In this summer peacefulness
Silence better tells his tale.

Your free senses have discerned,
　　Ere his stamm'ring lips can part,
　　That, for which but heart to heart
Knows a language, yet unlearned.

Lean, my Dearest, lean your head
　　Quietly against me: lay
　　Little hand in mine, to say,
'Thus, indeed, the heart is sped.'

Ah! a cloud across the sun!
　　Ah! a chill within the breeze!
　　Ah! a shiver through the trees!
And the flower-land is dun!

Nothing! see the light return,
　　Clearer from the gray eclipse!
　　And the smile about your lips
Tells a spirit's unconcern.

Foolish, verily, was I,
　　Dreaming you should thus divine
　　Secrets of this heart of mine.
Love for you comes by-and-by.

Here, enough, to-day you feel
    This bland summer hour's content;
    Magic music, colour, scent,
Through your happy senses steal.

Only, Dearest, lean your head
    Quietly against me. So!
    Leave me, when these moments go,
Ah! what memories instead!

SELWYN IMAGE
Poems and Carols (1894)

O MORS! QUAM AMARA EST MEMORIA TUA HOMINI PACEM HABENTI IN SUBSTANTIIS SUIS

Exceeding sorrow
    Consumeth my sad heart!
Because to-morrow
    We must depart,
Now is exceeding sorrow
    All my part!

Give over playing,
    Cast thy viol away:
Merely laying
    Thine head my way:
Prithee, give over playing,
    Grave or gay.

Be no word spoken;
    Weep nothing: let a pale
Silence, unbroken
    Silence prevail!

Prithee, be no word spoken,
  Lest I fail!

Forget to-morrow!
  Weep nothing: only lay
In silent sorrow
  Thine head my way:
Let us forget to-morrow,
  This one day!

ERNEST DOWSON
Verses (1896)

TRANSITION

A little while to walk with thee, dear child;
  To lean on thee my weak and weary head;
Then evening comes: the winter sky is wild,
  The leafless trees are black, the leaves long dead.

A little while to hold thee and to stand,
  By harvest-fields of bending golden corn:
Then the predestined silence, and thine hand,
  Lost in the night, long and weary and forlorn.

A little while to love thee, scarcely time
  To love thee well enough; then time to part,
To fare through wintry fields alone and climb
  The frozen hills, not knowing where thou art.

Short summer-time and then, my heart's desire,
  The winter and the darkness: one by one
The roses fall, the pale roses expire
Beneath the slow decadence of the sun.

ERNEST DOWSON
Decorations (1899)

SONG from *THE TRAGIC MARY*

Ah me, if I grew sweet to man
It was but as a rose that can
No longer keep the breath that heaves
And swells among its folded leaves.

The pressing fragrance would unclose
The flower, and I became a rose,
That unimpeachable and fair
Planted its sweetness in the air.

No art I used men's love to draw;
I lived but by my being's law,
As roses are by heaven designed
To bring the honey to the wind.

MICHAEL FIELD
Underneath the Bough (revised edition 1893)

RETURN OF THE TROOPS

The town is very gay to-day,
    And down our busy street
Flags wave, and all the balconies
    Are filled, our men to greet.

One night, not very long ago,
    I heard them marching down
To where their ship lay, and the sound
    So filled the silent town

With farewell voices that I wept
    To know no word or deed
Of mine had stirred the sleeping night,
    To bid our men God-speed.

The town is very gay to-day,
    And in our busy street,
My eyes are dim with tears for those
    I neither sped nor greet.

DOLLIE RADFORD
A Light Load (1891)

A SHROPSHIRE LAD

22

The street sounds to the soldiers' tread,
    And out we troop to see:
A single redcoat turns his head,
    He turns and looks at me.

My man, from sky to sky's so far,
    We never crossed before;
Such leagues apart the world's ends are,
    We're like to meet no more;

What thoughts at heart have you and I
    We cannot stop to tell;
But dead or living, drunk or dry,
    Soldier, I wish you well.

A. E. HOUSMAN
A Shropshire Lad (1896)

THE TRAVELLING COMPANION

Into the silence of the empty night
I went, and took my scornèd heart with me,
And all the thousand eyes of heaven were bright;
But Sorrow came and led me back to thee.

I turned my weary eyes towards the sun,
Out of the leaden East like smoke came he.
I laughed and said, 'The night is past and done';
But Sorrow came and led me back to thee.

I turned my face towards the rising moon,
Out of the south she came most sweet to see,
She smiled upon my eyes that loathed the noon;
But Sorrow came and led me back to thee.

I bent my eyes upon the summer land,
And all the painted fields were ripe for me,
And every flower nodded to my hand;
But Sorrow came and led me back to thee.

O Love! O Sorrow! O desired Despair!
I turn my feet towards the boundless sea,
Into the dark I go and heed not where,
So that I come again at last to thee.

LORD ALFRED DOUGLAS
The City of the Soul (1899)

IDEALISM

I know the woman has no soul, I know
    The woman has no possibilities
    Of soul or mind or heart, but merely is
The masterpiece of flesh: well, be it so.
It is her flesh that I adore; I go
   Thirsting afresh to drain her empty kiss.
   I know she cannot love: it is not this
My vanquished heart implores in overthrow.
Tyrannously I crave, I crave alone,
   Her perfect body, Earth's most eloquent
    Music, divinest human harmony;
   Her body now a silent instrument,
    That 'neath my touch shall wake and make for me
The strains I have but dreamed of, never known.

ARTHUR SYMONS
London Nights (2nd edition 1897)

῎Ερος δ'αὖτε …

   Crimson nor yellow roses, nor
   The savour of the mounting sea
   Are worth the perfume I adore
   That clings to thee.

   The languid-headed lilies tire,
   The changeless waters weary me.
   I ache with passionate desire
   Of thine and thee.

There are but these things in the world –
Thy mouth of fire,
Thy breasts, thy hands, thy hair upcurled,
And my desire!

THEODORE WRATISLAW
Orchids (1896)

STELLA MARIS

Why is it I remember yet
You, of all women one has met
In random wayfare, as one meets
The chance romances of the streets,
The Juliet of a night? I know
Your heart holds many a Romeo.
And I, who call to mind your face
In so serene a pausing-place,
Where the bright pure expanse of sea,
The shadowy shore's austerity,
Seem a reproach to you and me,
I too have sought on many a breast
The ecstasy of love's unrest,
I too have had my dreams, and met
(Ah me!) how many a Juliet.
Why is it, then, that I recall
You, neither first nor last of all?
For, surely as I see to-night
The phantom of the lighthouse light,
Against the sky, across the bay,
Fade, and return, and fade away,
So surely do I see your eyes
Out of the empty night arise.

Child, you arise and smile to me
Out of the night, out of the sea,
The Nereid of a moment there,
And is it seaweed in your hair?

O lost and wrecked, how long ago,
Out of the drowning past, I know
You come to call me, come to claim
My share of your delicious shame.
Child, I remember, and can tell
One night we loved each other well,
And one night's love, at least or most,
Is not so small a thing to boast.
You were adorable, and I
Adored you to infinity,
That nuptial night too briefly borne
To the oblivion of morn.
Ah! no oblivion, for I feel
Your lips deliriously steal
Along my neck, and fasten there;
I feel the perfume of your hair,
I feel your breast that heaves and dips,
Desiring my desirous lips,
And that ineffable delight
When souls turn bodies, and unite
In the intolerable, the whole
Rapture of the embodied soul.

That joy was ours, we passed it by;
You have forgotten me, and I
Remember you thus strangely, won
An instant from oblivion.
And I, remembering, would declare
That joy, not shame, is ours to share,

Joy that we had the frank delight
To choose the chances of one night,
Out of vague nights, and days at strife,
So infinitely full of life.
What shall it profit me to know
Your heart holds many a Romeo?
Why should I grieve, though I forget
How many another Juliet?
Let us be glad to have forgot
That roses fade, and loves are not,
As dreams, immortal, though they seem
Almost as real as a dream.
It is for this I see you rise,
A wraith, with starlight in your eyes,
Where calm hours move, for such a mood
Solitude out of solitude;
For this, for this, you come to me
Out of the night, out of the sea.

ARTHUR SYMONS
London Nights (2nd edition 1897)

NON SUM QUALIS ERAM BONAE
SUB REGNO CYNARAE

Last night, ah, yesternight, betwixt her lips and mine
There fell thy shadow, Cynara! thy breath was shed
Upon my soul between the kisses and the wine;
And I was desolate and sick of an old passion,
    Yea, I was desolate and bowed my head:
I have been faithful to thee, Cynara! in my fashion.

All night upon mine heart I felt her warm heart beat,
Night-long within mine arms in love and sleep she lay;
Surely the kisses of her bought red mouth were sweet;

But I was desolate and sick of an old passion,
　　When I awoke and found the dawn was gray:
I have been faithful to thee, Cynara! in my fashion.

I have forgot much, Cynara! gone with the wind,
Flung roses, roses riotously with the throng,
Dancing, to put thy pale, lost lilies out of mind;
But I was desolate and sick of an old passion,
　　Yea, all the time, because the dance was long:
I have been faithful to thee, Cynara! in my fashion.

I cried for madder music and for stronger wine,
But when the feast is finished and the lamps expire,
Then falls thy shadow, Cynara! the night is thine;
And I am desolate and sick of an old passion,
　　Yea hungry for the lips of my desire:
I have been faithful to thee, Cynara! in my fashion.

ERNEST DOWSON
Verses (1896)

MORBIDEZZA

White girl, your flesh is lilies,
Grown 'neath a frozen moon,
So still is
The rapture of your swoon
Of whiteness, snow or lilies.

The virginal revealment,
Your bosom's wavering slope,
Concealment,
'Neath fainting heliotrope,
Of whitest white's revealment,

Is like a bed of lilies,
A jealous-guarded row,
Whose will is
Simply chaste dreams : – but oh,
The alluring scent of lilies !

ARTHUR SYMONS
Silhouettes (2nd edition 1896)

THE DESTROYER OF A SOUL

I hate you with a necessary hate.
First, I sought patience : passionate was she :
My patience turned in very scorn of me,
That I should dare forgive a sin so great,
As this, through which I sit disconsolate ;
Mourning for that live soul, I used to see ;
Soul of a saint, whose friend I used to be :
Till you came by ! a cold, corrupting, fate.

Why come you now ? You, whom I cannot cease
With pure and perfect hate to hate ? Go, ring
The death-bell with a deep, triumphant toll !
Say you, my friend sits by me still ? Ah, peace !
Call you this thing my friend ? this nameless thing ?
This living body, hiding its dead soul ?

LIONEL JOHNSON
Poems (1895)

AGAINST MY LADY BURTON:
ON HER BURNING THE LAST
WRITING OF HER DEAD HUSBAND

'To save his soul', whom narrowly she loved
She did this deed of everlasting shame,
For devils' laughter; and was soulless proved
Heaping dishonour on her scholar's name.
Her lean distrust awoke when he was dead;
Dead, hardly cold; whose life was worn away
In scholarship's high service; from his head
She lightly tore his ultimate crown of bay.
His masterpiece, the ripe fruit of his age,
In art's despite she gave the hungry flame;
Smiled at the death of each laborious page,
Which she read only by the light of shame.
Dying he trusted her: him dead she paid
Most womanly, destroying his life's prize:
So Judas decently his Lord betrayed
With deep dishonour wrought in love's disguise.
With deep dishonour, for her jealous heart
His whole life's work, with light excuse put by
For love of him, or haply, hating art.
Oh Love be this, let us curse Love and die.
Nay! Love forgive: could such a craven thing
Love anywhere? but let her name pass down
Dishonoured through the ages, who did fling
To the rank scented mob a sage's crown,
And offered Fame, Love, Honour, mincingly
To her one God – sterile Propriety!

ERNEST DOWSON
Written 1891
Text from *The Poetical Works of Ernest Dowson* (1967)

THE PRICE

Terrible is the price
 Of beginning anew, of birth;
For Death has loaded dice.

Men hurry and hide like mice;
 But they cannot evade the Earth,
And Life, Death's fancy price.

A blossom once or twice,
 Love lights on Summer's hearth;
But Winter loads the dice.

In jangling shackles of ice,
 Ragged and bleeding, Mirth
Pays the Piper's price.

The dance is done in a trice:
 Death belts his bony girth;
And struts, and rattles his dice.

Let Virtue play or Vice,
 Beside his sombre firth
Life is the lowest price
Death wins with loaded dice.

JOHN DAVIDSON
The Last Ballad (1899)

AD CINERARIUM

Who in this small urn reposes,
    Celt or Roman, man or woman,
Steel of steel, or rose of roses?

Whose the dust set rustling slightly,
    In its hiding-place abiding,
When this urn is lifted lightly?

Sure some mourner deemed immortal
    What thou holdest and enfoldest,
Little house without a portal!

When the artificers had slowly
    Formed thee, turned thee, sealed thee, burned thee,
Freighted with thy freightage holy,

Sure he thought there's no forgetting
    All the sweetness and completeness
Of his rising, of her setting,

And so bade them grave no token,
    Generation, age, or nation,
On thy round side still unbroken; –

Let them score no cypress verses,
    Funeral glories, prayers, or stories,
Mourner's tears, or mourner's curses,

Round thy brown rim time hath polished, –
    Left thee dumbly cold and comely
As some shrine of gods abolished.

Ah, 'twas well! It scarcely matters
   What is sleeping in the keeping
Of this house of human tatters, –

Steel of steel, or rose of roses,
   Man or woman, Celt or Roman,
If but soundly he reposes!

VICTOR PLARR
In the Dorian Mood (1896)

A DREAM OF DEATH

I dreamed that one had died in a strange place
Near no accustomed hand;
And they had nailed the boards above her face,
The peasants of that land,
And, wondering, planted by her solitude
A cypress and a yew:
I came, and wrote upon a cross of wood,
Man had no more to do:
She was more beautiful than thy first love,
This lady by the trees:
And gazed upon the mournful stars above,
And heard the mournful breeze.

W. B. YEATS
Poems (1899)

VIGILANTIBUS

When Morning, with a hundred wings,
   Broke through the curtain-chink; and wept
   The earth, at what the day-break brings:
     The body slept.

A little yet the early sky,
With gold and blue, shall be astir
For you; while you are passing by:
    But not for her.

Go! let the voices of your feet
Speak thoughts beyond the tongue's control;
For now, in ways where all things meet,
    Now sleeps the soul.

Go! nor forget the steadfast gaze,
That, loosed in Death, hath pierced the night
Of the great mystery of our days,
    With eyes of light.

HERBERT HORNE
Diversi Colores (1891)

EPITAPHIUM CITHARISTRIAE

Stand not uttering sedately
    Trite oblivious praise above her!
Rather say you saw her lately
    Lightly kissing her last lover:

Whisper not, 'There is a reason
    Why we bring her no white blossom:'
Since the snowy bloom's in season
    Strow it on her sleeping bosom:

Oh, for it would be a pity
    To o'erpraise her or to flout her:
She was wild, and sweet, and witty –
    Let's not say dull things about her.

VICTOR PLARR
In the Dorian Mood (1896)

THE LAST MUSIC

Calmly, breathe calmly all your music, maids!
Breathe a calm music over my dead queen.
All your lives long, you have nor heard, nor seen,
Fairer than she, whose hair in sombre braids
    With beauty overshades
    Her brow, broad and serene.

Surely she hath lain so an hundred years:
Peace is upon her, old as the world's heart.
Breathe gently, music! Music done, depart:
And leave me in her presence to my tears,
    With music in mine ears;
    For sorrow hath its art.

Music, more music, sad and slow! she lies
Dead: and more beautiful, than early morn.
Discrowned am I, and of her looks forlorn:
Alone vain memories immortalize
    The way of her soft eyes,
    Her musical voice low-borne.

The balm of gracious death now laps her round,
As once life gave her grace beyond her peers.
Strange! that I loved this lady of the spheres,
To sleep by her at last in common ground:
    When kindly sleep hath bound
    Mine eyes, and sealed mine ears.

Maidens! make a low music: merely make
Silence a melody, no more. This day,
She travels down a pale and lonely way:

Now, for a gentle comfort, let her take
    Such music, for her sake,
    As mourning love can play.

Holy my queen lies in the arms of death:
Music moves over her still face, and I
Lean breathing love over her. She will lie
In earth thus calmly, under the wind's breath:
    The twilight wind, that saith:
    Rest! worthy found, to die.

LIONEL JOHNSON
Poems (1895)

AEDH PLEADS WITH THE
ELEMENTAL POWERS

The Powers whose name and shape no living creature knows
Have pulled the Immortal Rose;
And though the Seven Lights bowed in their dance and wept,
The Polar Dragon slept,
His heavy rings uncoiled from glimmering deep to deep:
When will he wake from sleep?

Great Powers of falling wave and wind and windy fire,
With your harmonious choir
Encircle her I love and sing her into peace,
That my old care may cease;
Unfold your flaming wings and cover out of sight
The nets of day and night.

Dim Powers of drowsy thought, let her no longer be
Like the pale cup of the sea,

When winds have gathered and sun and moon burned dim
Above its cloudy rim;
But let a gentle silence wrought with music flow
Whither her footsteps go.

W. B. YEATS
The Wind Among the Reeds (1899)

6. Fire from France

FIRE FROM FRANCE

(All the poems in this section are translations.)

In the title of his *English Poems* (1892) Richard Le Gallienne declared his position against the French influence; ironically so, for he had earlier exemplified the power of that influence when he introduced the 'Le' into his name. Now he was stolidly English, and in the poem 'To the Reader' complained to England,

> not of thee this new voice in our ears,
> Music of France that once was of the spheres;
> And not of thee these strange green flowers that spring
> From daisy roots and seem to bear a sting.

Certainly, for good or ill, France was the most potent foreign influence on English writing, both in style and content, at the end of the nineteenth century. Davidson in his *Fleet Street Eclogues* wrote that 'Some have stolen fire from France'. *The Times* called the first volume of *The Yellow Book* a 'combination of English rowdyism and French lubricity'. Words and phrases came from France: *épater le bourgeois*, decadence, *fin de siècle*, *art nouveau;* many moralists felt that the degenerate morals that they claimed to see came from there too and should be sent back. Lord Alfred Douglas published his *Poèmes* (1896) in both French and English. Even Lionel Johnson wrote an article on contemporary French poetic practice. Both *The Yellow Book* and *The Savoy* published poems in French, the latter translating Verlaine's account of his visit to England where his lecture was heard by most of the aspiring poets. Even when feelings against the French influence ran highest, *The Savoy* under

Symons's editorship continued to stress the importance of French literature.

The most frequently remembered of the French writers were Gautier, Baudelaire, Huysmans, Verlaine and Mallarmé. The general effect of their influence was a reinforcement of ideas drawn from English sources, and the stimulus of new ideas both of form and content.

Of the translators, Symons was the most influential since he backed up his translations with perceptive essays on contemporary, usually French, literature. His influence was great on both Eliot and Yeats. Eliot remarked that but for reading Symons (he was referring to *The Symbolist Movement in Literature*) he would never have read Laforgue and the other Symbolists. Yeats seems to have regarded Symons primarily as a translator, since his three selections of his work for *The Oxford Book of Modern Verse* are all translations.

The poets were not blind to work in countries other than France. If most of the writers understood French, many knew German, though they may have viewed it, as Lionel Johnson did, as a 'gross tongue, partially redeemed by Heine'. In *Italian Lyrists of To-day* (1893), G. A. Greene, a member of the Rhymers' Club, translated over thirty contemporary Italian poets, including the young d'Annunzio, the subject of one of Symons's essays and a poet who demonstrates the pervasiveness of the French influence.

For such as Lionel Johnson the classics came first, and several poems demonstrate a love of Latin, not always the late Latin which des Esseintes favoured and whose 'patches of rouge' had more charm for Mallarmé 'than the rosy flesh of youth'. Johnson, also a member of the Rhymers' Club, which was predominantly Irish, also fell under the influence of Celtic literature, though the pale light of the Celtic Twilight shows more diffused than in direct translation.

CHARLEVILLE

The square, with gravel paths and shabby lawns.
Correct, the trees and flowers repress their yawns.
The tradesman brings his favourite conceit,
To air it, while he stifles with the heat.

In the kiosk, the military band.
The shakos nod the time of the quadrilles.
The flaunting dandy strolls about the stand.
The notary, half unconscious of his seals.

On the green seats, small groups of grocermen,
Absorbed, their sticks scooping a little hole
Upon the path, talk market prices; then
Take up a cue: I think, upon the whole . . .

The loutish roughs are larking on the grass.
The sentimental trooper, with a rose
Between his teeth, seeing a baby, grows
More tender, with an eye upon the nurse.

Unbuttoned, like a student, I follow
A couple of girls along the chestnut row.
They know I am following, for they turn and laugh,
Half impudent, half shy, inviting chaff.

I do not say a word. I only stare
At their round, fluffy necks. I follow where
The shoulders drop; I struggle to define
The subtle torso's hesitating line.

Only my rustling tread, deliberate, slow;
The rippled silence from the still leaves drips.
They think I am an idiot, they speak low;
– I feel faint kisses creeping on my lips.

JOHN GRAY
From the French of Arthur Rimbaud
Silverpoints (1893)

PANTOMIME

    Pierrot, no sentimental swain,
    Washes a pâté down again
      With furtive flagons, white and red.

    Cassandre, to chasten his content,
    Greets with a tear of sentiment
      His nephew disinherited.

    That blackguard of a Harlequin
    Pirouettes, and plots to win
      His Colombine that flits and flies.

    Colombine dreams, and starts to find
    A sad heart sighing in the wind,
      And in her heart a voice that sighs.

ARTHUR SYMONS
From the French of Paul Verlaine
Silhouettes (2nd edition 1896)

FANTOCHES

Scaramouche waves a threatening hand
To Pulcinella, and they stand,
   Two shadows, black against the moon.

The old doctor of Bologna pries
For simples with impassive eyes,
   And mutters o'er a magic rune.

The while his daughter, scarce half-dressed,
Glides slyly 'neath the trees, in quest
   Of her bold pirate lover's sail;

Her pirate from the Spanish main,
Whose passion thrills her in the pain
   Of the loud languorous nightingale.

ARTHUR SYMONS
From the French of Paul Verlaine
Silhouettes (2nd edition 1896)

FEMMES DAMNÉES

Like moody beasts they lie along the sands;
Look where the sky against the sea-rim clings:
Foot stretches out to foot, and groping hands
Have languors soft and bitter shudderings.

Some, smitten hearts with the long secrecies,
On velvet moss, deep in their bowers' ease,
Prattling the love of timid infancies,
Are tearing the green bark from the young trees.

Others, like sisters, slowly walk and grave;
By rocks that swarm with ghostly legions,
Where Anthony saw surging on the waves
The purple breasts of his temptations.

Some, by the light of crumbling, resinous gums,
In the still hollows of old pagan dens,
Call thee in aid to their deliriums
O Bacchus! cajoler of ancient pains.

And those whose breasts for scapulars are fain
Nurse under their long robes the cruel thong.
These, in dim woods, where huddling shadows throng,
Mix with the foam of pleasure tears of pain.

JOHN GRAY
From the French of Charles Baudelaire
Silverpoints (1893)

COLLOQUE SENTIMENTAL

Into the lonely park all frozen fast,
Awhile ago there were two forms who passed.

Lo, are their lips fallen and their eyes dead,
Hardly shall a man hear the words they said.

Into the lonely park, all frozen fast,
There came two shadows who recall the past.

'Dost thou remember our old ecstasy?' –
'Wherefore should I possess that memory?' –

'Doth thine heart beat at my sole name alway?
Still dost thou see my soul in visions?' 'Nay!' –

'They were fair days of joy unspeakable,
Whereon our lips were joined?' – 'I cannot tell.' –

'Were not the heavens blue, was not hope high?'
'Hope has fled vanquished down the darkling sky.' –

So through the barren oats they wanderèd,
And the night only heard the words they said.

ERNEST DOWSON
From the French of Paul Verlaine
Decorations (1899)

SPLEEN

Around were all the roses red,
The ivy all around was black.

Dear, so thou only move thine head,
Shall all mine old despairs awake!

Too blue, too tender was the sky,
The air too soft, too green the sea.

Always I fear, I know not why,
Some lamentable flight from thee.

I am so tired of holly-sprays
And weary of the bright box-tree,

Of all the endless country ways;
Of everything alas! save thee.

ERNEST DOWSON
From the French of Paul Verlaine
Decorations (1899)

SPLEEN

The roses every one were red,
And all the ivy leaves were black.

Sweet, do not even stir your head,
Or all of my despairs come back.

The sky is too blue, too delicate:
Too soft the air, too green the sea.

I fear – how long had I to wait! –
That you will tear yourself from me.

The shining box-leaves weary me,
The varnished holly's glistening,

The stretch of infinite country;
So, saving you, does everything.

JOHN GRAY
From the French of Paul Verlaine
Silverpoints (1893)

LA DESTRUCTION

The Devil stirs about me without rest,
And round me floats like noxious air and thin;
I breathe this poison-air which scalds my breast,
And fills me with desires of monstrous sin.

Knowing my love of Art, he sometimes takes
The shape of supple girls supremely fair;
And with a wily, canting lie he makes
My heated lips his shameful potions share.

Then far he leads me from the sight of God,
Crushed with fatigue, to where no man has trod –
To the vague, barren plains where silence sounds,

And hurls into my face his foul construction
Of slimy clothes, and gaping, putrid wounds,
And all the bleeding harness of Destruction!

VINCENT O'SULLIVAN
From the French of Charles Baudelaire
Poems (1896)

HARMONIE DU SOIR

Voici venir le temps

Now is the hour when, swinging in the breeze,
Each flower, like a censer, sheds its sweet.
The air is full of scents and melodies,
O languorous waltz! O swoon of dancing feet!

Each flower, like a censer, sheds its sweet,
The violins are like sad souls that cry,
O languorous waltz! O swoon of dancing feet!
A shrine of Death and Beauty is the sky.

The violins are like sad souls that cry,
Poor souls that hate the vast black night of Death;
A shrine of Death and Beauty is the sky.
Drowned in red blood, the Sun gives up his breath.

This soul that hates the vast black night of Death
Takes all the luminous past back tenderly.
Drowned in red blood, the Sun gives up his breath.
Thine image like a monstrance shines in me.

LORD ALFRED DOUGLAS
From the French of Charles Baudelaire
The City of the Soul (1899)

JOYFUL DEATH

In a snail-covered earth and rich and deep
    I will dig out for mine own self my grave,
Where I can throw my old tired bones and sleep
    Forgetful as a shark upon the wave.

I hate both wills and tombs; rather, God knows,
    Than ask the world one tear upon my name,
Living, I would far gladlier bid the crows
    Suck out the blood from my uncleanly frame.

O worms! black friends who may not hear or see,
There comes to you a dead man glad and free!
Philosophers! Wise sons of rottenness,

Unpitying crawl from feet to ruined head
And tell me if any pain remains for this
Old soulless body dead among the dead!

THEODORE WRATISLAW
From the French of Charles Baudelaire
Love's Memorial (1892)

PRELUDE

As from corrupted flesh the over-bold
Young vines in dense luxuriance rankly grow,
And strange weird plants their horrid buds unfold
O'er the foul rotting of a corpse below;

As spreading crimson flowers with centred gold
Like the fresh blood of recent wounds o'erflow,
Where vile enormous chrysalids are rolled
In the young leaves, and cruel blossoms blow:

E'en so within my heart malignant flowers
Of verse swell forth: the leaves in fearful gloom
Exhale a sinister scent of human breath.

Lured by the radiance of the blood-red bowers,
The unconscious hand is stretched to pluck the bloom,
And the sharp poison fills the veins with death.

G. A. GREENE
From the Italian of Gabriele d'Annunzio
Italian Lyrists of To-day (1893)

SEA-WIND

The flesh is sad, alas! and all the books are read.
Flight, only flight! I feel that birds are wild to tread
The floor of unknown foam, and to attain the skies!
Nought, neither ancient gardens mirrored in the eyes,
Shall hold this heart that bathes in waters its delight,
O nights! nor yet my waking lamp, whose lonely light
Shadows the vacant paper, whiteness profits best,
Nor the young wife who rocks her baby on her breast.

I will depart! O steamer, swaying rope and spar,
Lift anchor for exotic lands that lie afar!
A weariness, outworn by cruel hopes, still clings
To the last farewell handkerchief's last beckonings!
And are not these, the masts inviting storms, not these
That an awakening wind bends over wrecking seas,
Lost, not a sail, a sail, a flowering isle, ere long?
But, O my heart, hear thou, hear thou the sailors' song!

ARTHUR SYMONS
From the French of Stéphane Mallarmé
Images of Good and Evil (1899)

CARMEN *CI*

By ways remote and distant waters sped,
Brother, to thy sad grave-side am I come,
That I may give the last gifts to the dead,
And vainly parley with thine ashes dumb:
Since she who now bestows and now denies
Hath ta'en thee, hapless brother, from mine eyes.

But lo! these gifts, the heirlooms of past years,
Are made sad things to grace thy coffin shell,
Take them, all drenchèd with a brother's tears,
And, brother, for all time, hail and farewell!

AUBREY BEARDSLEY
From the Latin of Catullus
In *The Savoy* (1896)

7. Poems and Ballads

POEMS AND BALLADS

THOUGH the organization of this section was designed to be loose enough to provide space for those poems which did not fall into the narrower categories of the other sections, the poems can be divided into two groups: those that deal, usually impressionistically, with traditional subject matter, and those written in the ballad tradition.

The impressions record, with the expected exception of one of Symons's poems, what John Gray calls 'the strait allure of simple things'. The love of the city was not so strong as to exclude all natural beauty; indeed, Yeats's 'Innisfree', among the most famous poems of nostalgia for the simple life, comes directly out of his homesickness in the midst of Fleet Street. Even Symons in 'A Causerie from a Castle in Ireland'[1] wrote that 'if I lived here too long I should forget that I am a Londoner and remember that I am a Cornishman. . . . I must come back to London; for I have perceived the insidious danger of idealism ever since I came to these ascetic regions.' Nature must always possess something of that attraction which Housman so beautifully, and in appearance so simply, caught.

The style of these poems is not that of the earlier Victorians. Under the influence of Pater, who wrote that for Rossetti the 'first condition of the poetic way of seeing and presenting things is particularization',[2] poets began to aim at exactly fixing the impression, in catching, like the later Degas, mood without narrative. Yeats explained that 'the revolt against Victorianism meant to the young poet a revolt

1. In *The Savoy*, Volume 6.
2. *Appreciations*.

against irrelevant descriptions of nature, the scientific and moral discursiveness of *In Memoriam* ... the political eloquence of Swinburne, the psychological curiosity of Browning, and the poetical diction of everybody'. 'For in truth,' Pater had written in *Appreciations*, 'all art does but consist in the removal of surplusage.' The precision and detail of these poems, in many ways like that striving for exactness of another of Pater's pupils, Gerard Manley Hopkins, is what resulted. Some of the features that Symons in 'The Decadent Movement in Literature' saw as elements of that style describe effectively Hopkins's attempts to depict the last fine shade: 'an intense self-consciousness, a restless curiosity in research, an over-subtilizing refinement upon refinement'. The clarity of the impression is also in a sense Imagistic. Pound praised the pure Imagism of Johnson's line from 'April', 'Clear lie the fields, and fade into blue air', and it is the 'nineties poets who began, as Yeats recorded, 'that search for hard subject-matter'.[3]

The ballad is a more specific but still a fairly loose form, large enough to include writers as different as Wilde, Kipling, and Housman, each of whom included an execution among his subjects ('The Ballad of Reading Gaol', 'Danny Deever', and *A Shropshire Lad*: 9). And Yeats and Davidson, despite their fierce mutual dislike, found parallel themes in 'The Ballad of Father Gilligan' and 'A Ballad of a Nun'. The ballad tends to imply traditional subject matter, the heroic event, the national myth, even the melodramatic story, and it is not surprising that Yeats, an Irishman, Davidson, a Scot, and the more jingoistic of the English poets wrote ballads.

Anthologies can usually afford to be kinder to lyric poets than to writers of ballads, and those ballads I include do

3. *The Oxford Book of Modern Verse.*

little more than suggest the production in this popular genre; for I omit some of the best known story-poems that come from this period, Newbolt's 'Drake's Drum' and 'He Fell Among Thieves', Kipling's 'Ballad of East and West' and 'The Road to Mandalay', and Wilde's ballad.

AT DIEPPE

AFTER SUNSET

The sea lies quieted beneath
   The after-sunset flush
That leaves upon the heaped grey clouds
   The grape's faint purple blush.

Pale, from a little space in heaven
   Of delicate ivory,
The sickle-moon and one gold star
   Look down upon the sea.

ARTHUR SYMONS
Silhouettes (2nd edition 1896)

A SHROPSHIRE LAD

2

Loveliest of trees, the cherry now
Is hung with bloom along the bough,
And stands about the woodland ride
Wearing white for Eastertide.

Now, of my threescore years and ten,
Twenty will not come again,
And take from seventy springs a score,
It only leaves me fifty more.

And since to look at things in bloom
Fifty springs are little room,
About the woodlands I will go
To see the cherry hung with snow.

A. E. HOUSMAN
A Shropshire Lad (1896)

PASTEL

The light of our cigarettes
   Went and came in the gloom:
   It was dark in the little room.

Dark, and then, in the dark,
   Sudden, a flash, a glow,
   And a hand and a ring I know.

And then, through the dark, a flush
   Ruddy and vague, the grace –
   A rose – of her lyric face.

ARTHUR SYMONS
Silhouettes (2nd edition 1896)

THE LAKE ISLE OF INNISFREE

I will arise and go now, and go to Innisfree,
And a small cabin build there, of clay and wattles made;
Nine bean rows will I have there, a hive for the honey bee,
And live alone in the bee-loud glade.

And I shall have some peace there, for peace comes dropping
   slow,
Dropping from the veils of the morning to where the cricket
   sings;
There midnight's all a glimmer, and noon a purple glow,
And evening full of the linnet's wings.

I will arise and go now, for always night and day
I hear lake water lapping with low sounds by the shore;
While I stand on the roadway, or on the pavements gray,
I hear it in the deep heart's core.

W. B. YEATS
Poems (1899)

APRIL

A pleasant heat breathes off the scented grass,
   From bright green blades, and shining daisies:
Now give we joy, who sometime cried, Alas!
Now set we forth our melodies, and sing
   Soft praises to the spring,
      Musical praises.

The flying winds are lovely with the sun:
   Now all in sweet and dainty fashion
Goes life: for royal seasons are begun.
Now each new day and each new promise add
   Fresh cause of being glad,
      With vernal passion.

Few leaves upon the branches dare the spring:
   But many buds are making ready,
Trusting the sun, their perfect summer king.
Likewise we put away our wintry cares:
   We hear but happy airs;
      Our hopes are steady.

John Gray

Cold were the crystal rivers, bitter cold;
  And snows upon the iron mountains;
And withering leaves upon the trodden mould.
Hark to the crystal voices of the rills,
  Falling among the hills,
    From secret fountains!

Long not for June with roses: nor for nights
  Loud with tumultuary thunder:
Those hours wax heavy with their fierce delights.
But April is all bright, and gives us first,
  Before the roses burst,
    Her joy and wonder.

Clear lie the fields, and fade into blue air:
  Here, sweet concerted birds are singing
Around this lawn of sweet grass, warm and fair.
And holy music, through the waving trees,
  Comes gently down the breeze,
    Where bells are ringing.

LIONEL JOHNSON
Poems (1895)

POEM

Geranium, houseleek, laid in oblong beds
On the trim grass. The daisies' leprous stain
Is fresh. Each night the daisies burst again,
Though every day the gardener crops their heads.

A wistful child, in foul unwholesome shreds,
Recalls some legend of a daisy chain
That makes a pretty necklace. She would fain
Make one, and wear it, if she had some threads.

Sun, leprous flowers, foul child. The asphalt burns.
The garrulous sparrows perch on metal Burns.
Sing! Sing! they say, and flutter with their wings.
He does not sing, he only wonders why
He is sitting there. The sparrows sing. And I
Yield to the strait allure of simple things.

JOHN GRAY
Silverpoints (1893)

IN ROMNEY MARSH

As I went down to Dymchurch Wall,
    I heard the South sing o'er the land;
I saw the yellow sunlight fall
    On knolls where Norman churches stand.

And ringing shrilly, taut and lithe,
    Within the wind a core of sound,
The wire from Romney town to Hythe
    Alone its airy journey wound.

A veil of purple vapour flowed
    And trailed its fringe along the Straits;
The upper air like sapphire glowed;
    And roses filled Heaven's central gates.

Masts in the offing wagged their tops;
    The swinging waves pealed on the shore;
The saffron beach, all diamond drops
    And beads of surge, prolonged the roar.

As I came up from Dymchurch Wall,
    I saw above the Downs' low crest
The crimson brands of sunset fall,
    Flicker and fade from out the west.

Night sank: like flakes of silver fire
    The stars in one great shower came down;
Shrill blew the wind; and shrill the wire
    Rang out from Hythe to Romney town.

The darkly shining salt sea drops
    Streamed as the waves clashed on the shore;
The beach, with all its organ stops
    Pealing again, prolonged the roar.

JOHN DAVIDSON
Ballads and Songs (1894)

THE BADGE OF MEN

'In shuttered rooms let others grieve,
    And coffin thought in speech of lead;
I'll tie my heart upon my sleeve:
    It is the Badge of Men,' he said.

His friends forsook him: 'Who was he!'
    Even beggars passed him with a grin:
Physicians called it lunacy;
    And priests, the unpardonable sin.

He strove, he struck for standing-ground:
    They beat him humbled from the field;
For though his sword was keen, he found
    His mangled heart a feeble shield.

He slunk away, and sadly sought
    The wilderness – false friend of woe.
'Man is The Enemy,' he thought;
    But Nature proved a fiercer foe:

The vampire sucked, the vulture tore,
    And the old dragon left its den,
Agape to taste the thing he wore –
    The ragged, bleeding Badge of Men.

'Against the Fates there steads no charm,
    For every force takes its own part:
I'll wear a buckler on my arm,
    And in my bosom hide my heart!'

But in his bosom prisoned fast
    It pained him more than when it beat
Upon his sleeve; and so he cast
    His trouble to the ghouls to eat.

Back to the city, there and then
    He ran; and saw, through all disguise,
On every sleeve the Badge of Men:
    For truth appears to cruel eyes.

Straight with his sword he laid about,
    And hacked and pierced their hearts, until
The beaten terror-stricken rout
    Begged on their knees to know his will.

He said, 'I neither love nor hate;
    I would command in everything.'
They answered him, 'Heartless and great!
    Your slaves we are: be you our king!'

JOHN DAVIDSON
The Last Ballad (1899)

John Davidson

A BALLAD OF A NUN

From Eastertide to Eastertide
  For ten long years her patient knees
Engraved the stones – the fittest bride
  Of Christ in all the diocese.

She conquered every earthly lust;
  The abbess loved her more and more;
And, as a mark of perfect trust,
  Made her the keeper of the door.

High on a hill the convent hung,
  Across a duchy looking down,
Where everlasting mountains flung
  Their shadows over tower and town.

The jewels of their lofty snows
  In constellations flashed at night;
Above their crests the moon arose;
  The deep earth shuddered with delight.

Long ere she left her cloudy bed,
  Still dreaming in the orient land,
On many a mountain's happy head
  Dawn lightly laid her rosy hand.

The adventurous sun took Heaven by storm;
  Clouds scattered largesses of rain;
The sounding cities, rich and warm,
  Smouldered and glittered in the plain.

Sometimes it was a wandering wind,
    Sometimes the fragrance of the pine,
Sometimes the thought how others sinned,
    That turned her sweet blood into wine.

Sometimes she heard a serenade
    Complaining sweetly far away:
She said, 'A young man woos a maid';
    And dreamt of love till break of day.

Then would she ply her knotted scourge
    Until she swooned; but evermore
She had the same red sin to purge,
    Poor, passionate keeper of the door!

For still night's starry scroll unfurled,
    And still the day came like a flood:
It was the greatness of the world
    That made her long to use her blood.

In winter-time when Lent drew nigh,
    And hill and plain were wrapped in snow,
She watched beneath the frosty sky
    The nearest city nightly glow.

Like peals of airy bells outworn
    Faint laughter died above her head
In gusts of broken music borne:
    'They keep the Carnival,' she said.

Her hungry heart devoured the town:
    'Heaven save me by a miracle!
Unless God sends an angel down,
    Thither I go though it were Hell.'

She dug her nails deep in her breast,
  Sobbed, shrieked, and straight withdrew the bar:
A fledgling flying from the nest,
  A pale moth rushing to a star.

Fillet and veil in strips she tore;
  Her golden tresses floated wide;
The ring and bracelet that she wore
  As Christ's betrothed, she cast aside.

'Life's dearest meaning I shall probe;
  Lo! I shall taste of love at last!
Away!' She doffed her outer robe,
  And sent it sailing down the blast.

Her body seemed to warm the wind;
  With bleeding feet o'er ice she ran:
'I leave the righteous God behind;
  I go to worship sinful man.'

She reached the sounding city's gate;
  No question did the warder ask:
He passed her in: 'Welcome, wild mate!'
  He thought her some fantastic mask.

Half-naked through the town she went;
  Each footstep left a bloody mark;
Crowds followed her with looks intent;
  Her bright eyes made the torches dark.

Alone and watching in the street
  There stood a grave youth nobly dressed;
To him she knelt and kissed his feet;
  Her face her great desire confessed.

Straight to his house the nun he led:
    'Strange lady, what would you with me?'
'Your love, your love, sweet lord,' she said;
    'I bring you my virginity.'

He healed her bosom with a kiss;
    She gave him all her passion's hoard;
And sobbed and murmured ever, 'This
    Is life's great meaning, dear, my lord.

'I care not for my broken vow;
    Though God should come in thunder soon,
I am sister to the mountains now,
    And sister to the sun and moon.'

Through all the towns of Belmarie
    She made a progress like a queen.
'She is,' they said, 'whate'er she be,
    The strangest woman ever seen.

'From fairyland she must have come,
    Or else she is a mermaiden.'
Some said she was a ghoul, and some
    A heathen goddess born again.

But soon her fire to ashes burned;
    Her beauty changed to haggardness;
Her golden hair to silver turned;
    The hour came of her last caress.

At midnight from her lonely bed
    She rose, and said, 'I have had my will.'
The old ragged robe she donned, and fled
    Back to the convent on the hill.

Half-naked as she went before,
   She hurried to the city wall,
Unnoticed in the rush and roar
   And splendour of the carnival.

No question did the warder ask:
   Her ragged robe, her shrunken limb,
Her dreadful eyes! 'It is no mask;
   It is a she-wolf, gaunt and grim!'

She ran across the icy plain;
   Her worn blood curdled in the blast;
Each footstep left a crimson stain;
   The white-faced moon looked on aghast.

She said between her chattering jaws,
   'Deep peace is mine, I cease to strive;
Oh, comfortable convent laws,
   That bury foolish nuns alive!

'A trowel for my passing-bell,
   A little bed within the wall,
A coverlet of stones; how well
   I there shall keep the Carnival!'

Like tired bells chiming in their sleep,
   The wind faint peals of laughter bore;
She stopped her ears and climbed the steep,
   And thundered at the convent door.

It opened straight: she entered in,
   And at the wardress' feet fell prone:
'I come to purge away my sin;
   Bury me, close me up in stone.'

The wardress raised her tenderly;
　　She touched her wet and fast-shut eyes:
'Look, sister; sister, look at me;
　　Look; can you see through my disguise?'

She looked and saw her own sad face,
　　And trembled, wondering, 'Who art thou?'
'God sent me down to fill your place:
　　I am the Virgin Mary now.'

And with the word, God's mother shone:
　　The wanderer whispered, 'Mary, hail!'
The vision helped her to put on
　　Bracelet and fillet, ring and veil.

'You are sister to the mountains now,
　　And sister to the day and night;
Sister to God.' And on the brow
　　She kissed her thrice, and left her sight.

While dreaming in her cloudy bed,
　　Far in the crimson orient land,
On many a mountain's happy head
　　Dawn lightly laid her rosy hand.

JOHN DAVIDSON
Ballads and Songs (1894)

THE BALLAD OF FATHER GILLIGAN

　　The old priest Peter Gilligan
　　Was weary night and day;
　　For half his flock were in their beds,
　　Or under green sods lay.

Once, while he nodded on a chair,
At the moth-hour of eve,
Another poor man sent for him,
And he began to grieve.

'I have no rest, nor joy, nor peace,
'For people die and die';
And after cried he, 'God forgive!
'My body spake, not I!'

And then, half-lying on the chair
He knelt, prayed, fell asleep;
And the moth-hour went from the fields,
And stars began to peep.

They slowly into millions grew,
And leaves shook in the wind;
And God covered the world with shade,
And whispered to mankind.

Upon the time of sparrow chirp
When the moths came once more,
The old priest Peter Gilligan
Stood upright on the floor.

'Mavrone, mavrone! the man has died,
'While I slept on the chair';
He roused his horse out of its sleep,
And rode with little care.

He rode now as he never rode,
By rocky lane and fen;
The sick man's wife opened the door:
'Father! you come again!'

'And is the poor man dead?' he cried.
'He died an hour ago.'
The old priest Peter Gilligan
In grief swayed to and fro.

'When you were gone, he turned and died
'As merry as a bird.'
The old priest Peter Gilligan
He knelt him at that word.

'He who hath made the night of stars
'For souls, who tire and bleed,
'Sent one of His great angels down
'To help me in my need.

'He who is wrapped in purple robes,
'With planets in His care,
'Had pity on the least of things
'Asleep upon a chair.'

W. B. YEATS
Poems (1899)

A SHROPSHIRE LAD

9

On moonlit heath and lonesome bank
    The sheep beside me graze;
And yon the gallows used to clank
    Fast by the four cross ways.

A careless shepherd once would keep
    The flocks by moonlight there,[1]
And high amongst the glimmering sheep
    The dead man stood on air.

1. Hanging in chains was called keeping sheep by moonlight.

They hang us now in Shrewsbury jail:
    The whistles blow forlorn,
And trains all night groan on the rail
    To men that die at morn.

There sleeps in Shrewsbury jail to-night,
    Or wakes, as may betide,
A better lad, if things went right,
    Than most that sleep outside.

And naked to the hangman's noose
    The morning clocks will ring
A neck God made for other use
    Than strangling in a string.

And sharp the link of life will snap,
    And dead on air will stand
Heels that held up as straight a chap
    As treads upon the land.

So here I'll watch the night and wait
    To see the morning shine,
When he will hear the stroke of eight
    And not the stroke of nine;

And wish my friend as sound a sleep
    As lads' I did not know,
That shepherded the moonlit sheep
    A hundred years ago.

A. E. HOUSMAN
A Shropshire Lad (1896)

ADMIRALS ALL

A SONG OF SEA KINGS

Effingham, Grenville, Raleigh, Drake,
 Here's to the bold and free!
Benbow, Collingwood, Byron, Blake,
 Hail to the Kings of the Sea!
Admirals all, for England's sake,
 Honour be yours and fame!
And honour, as long as waves shall break,
 To Nelson's peerless name!

> *Admirals all, for England's sake,*
> *Honour be yours and fame!*
> *And honour, as long as waves shall break,*
> *To Nelson's peerless name!*

Essex was fretting in Cadiz Bay
 With the galleons fair in sight;
Howard at last must give him his way,
 And the word was passed to fight.
Never was schoolboy gayer than he,
 Since holidays first began:
He tossed his bonnet to wind and sea,
 And under the guns he ran.

Drake nor devil nor Spaniard feared,
 Their cities he put to the sack;
He singed His Catholic Majesty's beard,
 And harried his ships to wrack.
He was playing at Plymouth a rubber of bowls
 When the great Armada came;
But he said, 'They must wait their turn, good souls,'
 And he stooped, and finished the game.

Fifteen sail were the Dutchmen bold,
   Duncan he had but two;
But he anchored them fast where the Texel shoaled,
   And his colours aloft he flew.
'I've taken the depth to a fathom,' he cried,
   'And I'll sink with a right good will:
For I know when we're all of us under the tide
   My flag will be fluttering still.'

Splinters were flying above, below,
   When Nelson sailed the Sound:
'Mark you, I wouldn't be elsewhere now,'
   Said he, 'for a thousand pound!'
The Admiral's signal bade him fly,
   But he wickedly wagged his head:
He clapped the glass to his sightless eye,
   And 'I'm damned if I see it!' he said.

Admirals all, they said their say,
   (The echoes are ringing still).
Admirals all, they went their way
   To the haven under the hill.
But they left us a kingdom none can take –
   The realm of the circling sea –
To be ruled by the rightful sons of Blake,
    And the Rodneys yet to be.

    Admirals all, for England's sake,
     Honour be yours and fame!
    And honour, as long as waves shall break,
     To Nelson's peerless name!

HENRY NEWBOLT
Admirals All, and Other Verses (1897)

THE BARBER

1

I dreamed I was a barber; and there went
Beneath my hand, oh! manes extravagant.
Beneath my trembling fingers, many a mask
Of many a pleasant girl. It was my task
To gild their hair, carefully, strand by strand;
To paint their eyebrows with a timid hand;
To draw a bodkin, from a vase of kohl,
Through the closed lashes; pencils from a bowl
Of sepia to paint them underneath;
To blow upon their eyes with a soft breath.
They lay them back and watched the leaping bands.

2

The dream grew vague. I moulded with my hands
The mobile breasts, the valley; and the waist
I touched; and pigments reverently placed
Upon their thighs in sapient spots and stains,
Beryls and crysolites and diaphanes,
And gems whose hot harsh names are never said.
I was a masseur; and my fingers bled
With wonder as I touched their awful limbs.

3

Suddenly, in the marble trough, there seems
O, last of my pale mistresses, Sweetness!
A twylipped scarlet pansie. My caress
Tinges thy steelgray eyes to violet.
Adown thy body skips the pit-a-pat
Of treatment once heard in a hospital
For plagues that fascinate, but half appal.

4

So, at the sound, the blood of me stood cold.
Thy chaste hair ripened into sullen gold.
The throat, the shoulders, swelled and were uncouth.
The breasts rose up and offered each a mouth.
And on the belly pallid blushes crept,
That maddened me, until I laughed and wept.

JOHN GRAY
Silverpoints (1893)

THE BALLAD OF A BARBER

Here is the tale of Carrousel,
The barber of Meridian Street.
He cut, and coiffed, and shaved so well,
That all the world was at his feet.

The King, the Queen, and all the Court,
To no one else would trust their hair,
And reigning belles of every sort
Owed their successes to his care.

With carriage and with cabriolet
Daily Meridian Street was blocked,
Like bees about a bright bouquet
The beaux about his doorway flocked.

Such was his art he could with ease
Curl wit into the dullest face;
Or to a goddess of old Greece
Add a new wonder and a grace.

All powders, paints, and subtle dyes,
And costliest scents that men distil,
And rare pomades, forgot their price
And marvelled at his splendid skill.

The curling irons in his hand
Almost grew quick enough to speak,
The razor was a magic wand
That understood the softest cheek.

Yet with no pride his heart was moved;
He was so modest in his ways!
His daily task was all he loved,
And now and then a little praise.

An equal care he would bestow
On problems simple or complex;
And nobody had seen him show
A preference for either sex.

How came it then one summer day,
Coiffing the daughter of the King,
He lengthened out the least delay
And loitered in his hairdressing?

The Princess was a pretty child,
Thirteen years old, or thereabout.
She was as joyous and as wild
As spring flowers when the sun is out.

Her gold hair fell down to her feet
And hung about her pretty eyes;
She was as lyrical and sweet
As one of Schubert's melodies.

Three times the barber curled a lock,
And thrice he straightened it again;
And twice the irons scorched her frock,
And twice he stumbled in her train.

His fingers lost their cunning quite,
His ivory combs obeyed no more;
Something or other dimmed his sight,
And moved mysteriously the floor.

He leant upon the toilet table,
His fingers fumbled in his breast;
He felt as foolish as a fable,
And feeble as a pointless jest.

He snatched a bottle of Cologne,
And broke the neck between his hands;
He felt as if he was alone,
And mighty as a king's commands.

The Princess gave a little scream,
Carrousel's cut was sharp and deep;
He left her softly as a dream
That leaves a sleeper to his sleep.

He left the room on pointed feet;
Smiling that things had gone so well.
They hanged him in Meridian Street.
You pray in vain for Carrousel.

AUBREY BEARDSLEY
In *The Savoy* (1896)

THE CAP AND BELLS

The jester walked in the garden:
The garden had fallen still;
He bade his soul rise upward
And stand on her window-sill.

It rose in a straight blue garment,
When owls began to call:
It had grown wise-tongued by thinking
Of a quiet and light footfall;

But the young queen would not listen;
She rose in her pale night gown;
She drew in the heavy casement
And pushed the latches down.

He bade his heart go to her,
When the owls called out no more;
In a red and quivering garment
It sang to her through the door.

It had grown sweet-tongued by dreaming,
Of a flutter of flower-like hair;
But she took up her fan from the table
And waved it off on the air.

'I have cap and bells' he pondered,
'I will send them to her and die;'
And when the morning whitened
He left them where she went by.

She laid them upon her bosom,
Under a cloud of her hair,
And her red lips sang them a love song:
Till stars grew out of the air.

She opened her door and her window,
And the heart and the soul came through,
To her right hand came the red one,
To her left hand came the blue.

They set up a noise like crickets,
A chattering wise and sweet,
And her hair was a folded flower
And the quiet of love in her feet.

W. B. YEATS
The Wind Among the Reeds (1899)

DAISY

Where the thistle lifts a purple crown
   Six foot out of the turf,
And the harebell shakes on the windy hill –
   O the breath of the distant surf ! –

The hills look over on the South,
   And southward dreams the sea ;
And, with the sea-breeze hand in hand,
   Came innocence and she.

Where 'mid the gorse the raspberry
   Red for the gatherer springs,
Two children did we stray and talk
   Wise, idle, childish things.

She listened with big-lipped surprise,
  Breast-deep mid flower and spine:
Her skin was like a grape, whose veins
  Run snow instead of wine.

She knew not those sweet words she spake,
  Nor knew her own sweet way;
But there's never a bird, so sweet a song
  Thronged in whose throat that day!

Oh, there were flowers in Storrington
  On the turf and on the spray;
But the sweetest flower on Sussex hills
  Was the Daisy-flower that day!

Her beauty smoothed earth's furrowed face!
  She gave me tokens three: —
A look, a word of her winsome mouth,
  And a wild raspberry.

A berry red, a guileless look,
  A still word, – strings of sand!
And yet they made my wild, wild heart
  Fly down to her little hand.

For standing artless as the air,
  And candid as the skies,
She took the berries with her hand,
  And the love with her sweet eyes.

The fairest things have fleetest end:
  Their scent survives their close,
But the rose's scent is bitterness
  To him that loved the rose!

She looked a little wistfully,
  Then went her sunshine way: —
The sea's eye had a mist on it,
  And the leaves fell from the day.

She went her unremembering way,
  She went and left in me
The pang of all the partings gone,
  And partings yet to be.

She left me marvelling why my soul
  Was sad that she was glad;
At all the sadness in the sweet,
  The sweetness in the sad.

Still, still I seemed to see her, still
  Look up with soft replies,
And take the berries with her hand,
  And the love with her lovely eyes.

Nothing begins, and nothing ends,
  That is not paid with moan;
For we are born in others' pain,
  And perish in our own.

FRANCIS THOMPSON
Poems (1893)

THE PRIEST OF LOVE

In Sicily in the days of art
  A painter prince held sway,
Who loved one lady with all his heart
  And dreamed of her night and day.

She was a girl of scarce thirteen,
  And he was but a youth;
Yet he sware none other should be his queen,
  And kept his oath with truth.

And still as she grew he built her a home,
  That the years less long might seem,
Out on an island, girt with the foam,
  Beautiful as a dream.

And he called the masters from every part,
  Of temper, and tint, and tone,
Who moulded in metal miraculous art,
  Or wrought it in colour or stone,

All carvers of wood and silver and gold,
  All weavers that loved the loom,
To make her a palace of perfect mould,
  And fill it with tender bloom.

And he sent for marbles out of the isles,
  Rose-red and white as snow,
And made a dome that shone for miles
  In the ruddy evening glow.

And the palace grew, and the maiden grew
  In stature and beauty and grace
Year by year – for shape and for hue,
  A wonderful woman's face.

And ever of marbles from far-off isles,
  Like music soft and slow,
Rose fluted pillars and fretted piles,
  And hung in the wave below,

With many a cupola poised above,
  And many a sculptured frieze,
That filled with anguish of hopeless love
  The amorous ocean breeze.

And he hung rich arras about the place,
  Wrought in a distant clime,
With love, and passion, and war, and the chase,
  And gods of the olden time;

And he steeped his brush in the hues of love,
  His soul in the poet's themes,
And filled the walls and the ceilings above
  With forms as fair as dreams;

And he melted his heart to heavenly hues,
  And bathed the grainèd glass
In burning reds and beautiful blues,
  And greens as soft as grass;

And he fetched rare marbles from far-off isles
  For the sculptors, as white as snow,
Who made them smile immortal smiles,
  With love immortal glow.

And the palace grew and the maiden grew
  In beauty side by side;
And when both were perfect in form and hue,
  And ready – the maiden died.

Then he shut himself up in the palace alone,
  With the statues and his despair,
And his young dead bride as cold as stone,
  And fired it, and perished there.

And the red flame shone to the far-off isles
    Over the ocean-flow,
And the sky was red for miles and miles,
    And the sea lay red below.

JOHN BARLAS
Songs of a Bayadere and Songs of a Troubadour (1893)

A BALLAD OF JOHN NICHOLSON

It fell in the year of Mutiny,
    At darkest of the night,
John Nicholson by Jalándhar came,
    On his way to Delhi fight.

And as he by Jalándhar came,
    He thought what he must do,
And he sent to the Rajah fair greeting,
    To try if he were true.

'God grant your Highness length of days,
    And friends when need shall be;
And I pray you send your Captains hither,
    That they may speak with me.'

On the morrow through Jalándhar town
    The Captains rode in state;
They came to the house of John Nicholson,
    And stood before the gate.

The chief of them was Mehtab Singh,
    He was both proud and sly;
His turban gleamed with rubies red,
    He held his chin full high.

He marked his fellows how they put
  Their shoes from off their feet;
'Now wherefore make ye such ado
  These fallen lords to greet?

'They have ruled us for a hundred years,
  In truth I know not how,
But though they be fain of mastery
  They dare not claim it now.'

Right haughtily before them all
  The durbar hall he trod,
With rubies red his turban gleamed,
  His feet with pride were shod.

They had not been an hour together,
  A scanty hour or so,
When Mehtab Singh rose in his place
  And turned about to go.

Then swiftly came John Nicholson
  Between the door and him,
With anger smouldering in his eyes,
  That made the rubies dim.

'You are over-hasty, Mehtab Singh,' –
  Oh, but his voice was low!
He held his wrath with a curb of iron
  That furrowed cheek and brow.

'You are over-hasty, Mehtab Singh,
  When that the rest are gone,
I have a word that may not wait
  To speak with you alone.'

The Captains passed in silence forth
   And stood the door behind;
To go before the game was played
   Be sure they had no mind.

But there within John Nicholson
   Turned him on Mehtab Singh,
'So long as the soul is in my body
   You shall not do this thing.

'Have ye served us for a hundred years
   And yet ye know not why?
We brook no doubt of our mastery,
   We rule until we die.

'Were I the one last Englishman
   Drawing the breath of life,
And you the master-rebel of all
   That stir this land to strife –

'Were I,' he said, 'but a Corporal,
   And you a Rajput King,
So long as the soul was in my body
   You should not do this thing.

'Take off, take off, those shoes of pride,
   Carry them whence they came;
Your Captains saw your insolence,
   And they shall see your shame.'

When Mehtab Singh came to the door
   His shoes they burned his hand,
For there in long and silent lines
   He saw the Captains stand.

When Mehtab Singh rode from the gate
   His chin was on his breast:
The Captains said, 'When the strong command
   Obedience is best.'

HENRY NEWBOLT
Admirals All (1897)

GUNGA DIN

You may talk o' gin and beer
When you're quartered safe out 'ere,
An' you're sent to penny-fights an' Aldershot it;
But when it comes to slaughter
You will do your work on water,
An' you'll lick the bloomin' boots of 'im that's got it.
Now in Injia's sunny clime,
Where I used to spend my time
A-servin' of 'Er Majesty the Queen,
Of all them blackfaced crew
The finest man I knew
Was our regimental bhisti, Gunga Din.
    He was 'Din! Din! Din!
  'You limpin' lump o' brick-dust, Gunga Din!
    'Hi! slippery *hitherao*!
    'Water, get it! *Panee lao!*[1]
  'You squidgy-nosed old idol, Gunga Din.'

The uniform 'e wore
Was nothin' much before,
An' rather less than 'arf o' that be'ind,
For a piece o' twisty rag
An' a goatskin water-bag
Was all the field-equipment 'e could find.

       1. Bring water swiftly.

When the sweatin' troop-train lay
In a sidin' through the day,
Where the 'eat would make your bloomin' eyebrows crawl,
We shouted 'Harry By!'[2]
Till our throats were bricky-dry,
Then we wopped 'im 'cause 'e couldn't serve us all.
  It was 'Din! Din! Din!
 'You 'eathen, where the mischief 'ave you been?
  'You put some *juldee*[3] in it
  'Or I'll *marrow*[4] you this minute
 'If you don't fill up my helmet, Gunga Din!'

'E would dot an' carry one
Till the longest day was done;
An' 'e didn't seem to know the use o' fear.
If we charged or broke or cut,
You could bet your bloomin' nut,
'E'd be waitin' fifty paces right flank rear.
With 'is mussick[5] on 'is back,
'E would skip with our attack,
An' watch us till the bugles made 'Retire,'
An' for all 'is dirty 'ide
'E was white, clear white, inside
When 'e went to tend the wounded under fire!
  It was 'Din! Din! Din!'
 With the bullets kickin' dust-spots on the green.
  When the cartridges ran out,
  You could hear the front-files shout,
 'Hi! ammunition-mules an' Gunga Din!'

I sha'n't forgit the night
When I dropped be'ind the fight
With a bullet where my belt-plate should 'a' been.

---

  2. Mr Atkins's equivalent for 'O brother'.
 3. Be quick. 4. Hit you. 5. Water-skin.

I was chokin' mad with thirst,
An' the man that spied me first
Was our good old grinnin', gruntin' Gunga Din.
'E lifted up my 'ead,
An' he plugged me where I bled,
An' 'e guv me 'arf-a-pint o' water-green:
It was crawlin' and it stunk,
But of all the drinks I've drunk,
I'm gratefullest to one from Gunga Din.
    It was 'Din! Din! Din!
  ''Ere's a beggar with a bullet through 'is spleen;
    ''E's chawin' up the ground,
    'An' 'e's kickin' all around:
  'For Gawd's sake git the water, Gunga Din!'

'E carried me away
To where a dooli lay,
An' a bullet come an' drilled the beggar clean.
'E put me safe inside,
An' just before 'e died,
'I 'ope you liked your drink,' sez Gunga Din.
So I'll meet 'im later on
At the place where 'e is gone –
Where it's always double drill and no canteen;
'E'll be squattin' on the coals
Givin' drink to poor damned souls,
An' I'll get a swig in hell from Gunga Din!
    Yes, Din! Din! Din!
  You Lazarushian-leather Gunga Din!
    Though I've belted you and flayed you,
    By the livin' Gawd that made you,
  You're a better man than I am, Gunga Din!

RUDYARD KIPLING
Barrack-Room Ballads (1892)

8. The Roses Fall

THE ROSES FALL

POET after poet seems to have found a complex comfort in the prospect of defeat, decline, and death, an attitude summed up by Mallarmé in his prose-poem 'Plainte d'Automne', where he says that 'I have loved all that is summed up in the word "fall"'. There were those who found this attitude objectionable, called it effeteness and effeminacy, and, as Yeats recalls Davidson did, demanded 'blood and guts'. But the feeling was nonetheless there, and the dying fall, the gentle, somewhat pallid languor, the exquisite boredom, are rightly thought of as characteristic of a good deal of 'nineties poetry. Many of the poets could have written of 'the tired taste and jaded sensibilities of our end of the century'. The description is in fact Richard Le Gallienne's, in a review of John Davidson's *The Wonderful Mission of Earl Lavender* (1895), the Proem to which ends

> Though our thoughts turn ever Doomwards,
>   Though our sun is well-nigh set,
> Though our Century totters tombwards,
>   We may laugh a little yet.

Even the laughter was a little wry. Max Beerbohm, seeing that Paterian experiences 'gave nothing but lassitude to those who had gained them through suffering', retired from the fray to rest on his laurels: 'I, who crave no knighthood, shall write no more. I shall write no more. Already I feel myself to be a trifle outmoded. I belong to the Beardsley period.' In the same year (1896) he published his *Works*, and reached the ripe age of twenty-four.

Other ages have affected melancholy, and other young men have felt this falling of the petals before the buds have opened, but in the 'nineties the feeling had a new importance. Its origins are complex. The century, whether one believed in the idea of centuries decaying or not, seemed to be dying in more than the simple numerical sense; the old queen was obviously near the end of her reign; frequent parallels were drawn between the Roman Empire in decline and the British Empire, politically, artistically, and morally; the old order was changing, the old gods falling. Some sort of cataclysmic event seemed to be looming ahead; events in retrospect seemed to be leading inevitably to the shattering changes of the First World War. The writers saw, in Frank Kermode's words in *The Sense of an Ending*, the '*fin de siècle*, where all the elements of the apocalyptic paradigm clearly co-exist'. Yeats, talking of Pater's *Marius the Epicurean* in *Autobiographies* wondered whether this book 'had not caused the disasters of my friends. It taught us to walk upon a rope, tightly stretched through serene air, and we were left to keep our feet upon a swaying rope in a storm.' Even the Celtic Renaissance encouraged the feeling of decline, directed as it was at the time by Arnold's essay 'On the Study of Celtic Literature'. Arnold characterized the Celtic sensibility by quoting from Ossian, 'They went forth to the war, but they always fell', and he felt fairly sure that English poetry got much of its melancholy from a Celtic source. This seems likely in the case of Lionel Johnson, determined to be Irish without much support from his ancestry, whose 'Mystic and Cavalier' obviously owes something to Arnold.

Wherever they originated, perhaps in the very sensibility that recognized them, 'the weariness, the fever and the fret' that Keats knew were still oppressing the poets of the 'nineties. But the 'wings of poesy' were there too, and it was ironically Hardy, who has been accused of a variety of gloomy philosophies, who saw at the very turn of the century, in a thrush instead of a nightingale, the possibilities of hope.

VITAE SUMMA BREVIS SPEM NOS
VETAT INCOHARE LONGAM

They are not long, the weeping and the laughter,
    Love and desire and hate:
I think they have no portion in us after
    We pass the gate.

They are not long, the days of wine and roses:
    Out of a misty dream
Our path emerges for a while, then closes
    Within a dream.

ERNEST DOWSON
Verses (1896)

THE SAD SHEPHERD

There was a man whom Sorrow named his friend,
And he, of his high comrade Sorrow dreaming,
Went walking with slow steps along the gleaming
And humming sands, where windy surges wend:
And he called loudly to the stars to bend
From their pale thrones and comfort him, but they
Among themselves laugh on and sing alway:
And then the man whom Sorrow named his friend
Cried out, *Dim sea, hear my most piteous story!*
The sea swept on and cried her old cry still,
Rolling along in dreams from hill to hill;
He fled the persecution of her glory

And, in a far-off, gentle valley stopping,
Cried all his story to the dewdrops glistening,
But naught they heard, for they are always listening,
The dewdrops, for the sound of their own dropping.
And then the man whom Sorrow named his friend,
Sought once again the shore, and found a shell
And thought, *I will my heavy story tell*
Till my own words, re-echoing, shall send
Their sadness through a hollow, pearly heart;
And my own tale again for me shall sing,
And my own whispering words be comforting
And lo! my ancient burden may depart.
Then he sang softly nigh the pearly rim;
But the sad dweller by the sea-ways lone
Changed all he sang to inarticulate moan
Among her wildering whirls, forgetting him.

W. B. YEATS
Poems (1899)

SORROW'S IMPORTUNITY

1

When Sorrow first came wailing to my door,
  April rehearsed the madrigal of May;
And, as I ne'er had seen her face before,
  I kept on singing, and she went her way.

2

When next came Sorrow, life was winged with scent
  Of glistening laurel and full-blossoming bay:
I asked, but understood not, what she meant,
  Offered her flowers, and she went her way.

3

When yet a third time Sorrow came, we met
    In the ripe silence of an Autumn day:
I gave her fruit I had gathered, and she ate,
    Then seemed to go unwillingly away.

4

When last came Sorrow, around barn and byre
    Wind-carven snow, the Year's white sepulchre, lay.
'Come in,' I said, 'and warm you by the fire.'
    And there she sits, and never goes away.

ALFRED AUSTIN
The Conversion of Winckelmann, and Other Poems
(2nd edition 1897)

PLAINTE ETERNELLE

The sun sinks down, the tremulous day-light dies,
    (Down their long shafts the weary sun-beams glide)
    The white-winged ships drift with the falling tide.
Come back, my love, with pity in your eyes!

The tall white ships drift with the falling tide.
    (Far, far away I hear the seamews' cries)
    Come back, my love, with pity in your eyes!
There is no room now in my heart for pride,

Come back, come back! with pity in your eyes,
    (The night is dark, the sea is fierce and wide)
    There is no room now in my heart for pride,
Though I become the scorn of all the wise.

I have no place now in my heart for pride.
   (The moon and stars have fallen from the skies)
   Though I become the scorn of all the wise,
Thrust, if you will, sharp arrows in my side.

Let me become the scorn of all the wise.
   (Out of the East I see the morning ride)
   Thrust, if you will, sharp arrows in my side,
Play with my tears and feed upon my sighs.

Wound me with swords, put arrows in my side,
   (On the white sea the haze of noon-day lies)
   Play with my tears and feed upon my sighs,
But come, my love, before my heart has died.

Drink my salt tears and feed upon my sighs,
   (Westward the evening goes with one red stride)
   Come back, my love, before my heart has died,
Down sinks the sun, the tremulous day-light dies.

Come back! my love, before my heart has died,
   (Out of the South I see the pale moon rise)
   Down sinks the sun, the tremulous day-light dies,
The white-winged ships drift with the falling tide.

LORD ALFRED DOUGLAS
Poèmes (1896)

THE ROSE OF BATTLE

Rose of all Roses, Rose of all the World!
The tall thought-woven sails, that flap unfurled
Above the tide of hours, trouble the air,
And God's bell buoyed to be the water's care;
While hushed from fear, or loud with hope, a band
With blown, spray-dabbled hair gather at hand.

The Roses Fall

Turn if you may from battles never done,
I call, as they go by me one by one,
Danger no refuge holds, and war no peace,
For him who hears love sing and never cease,
Beside her clean-swept hearth, her quiet shade;
But gather all for whom no love hath made
A woven silence, or but came to cast
A song into the air, and singing past
To smile on the pale dawn; and gather you,
Who have sought more than is in rain or dew,
Or in the sun and moon, or on the earth,
Or sighs amid the wandering, starry mirth,
Or comes in laughter from the sea's sad lips;
And wage God's battles in the long gray ships.
The sad, the lonely, the insatiable,
To these Old Night shall all her mystery tell;
God's bell has claimed them by the little cry
Of their sad hearts, that may not live nor die.

Rose of all Roses, Rose of all the World!
You, too, have come where the dim tides are hurled
Upon the wharves of sorrow, and heard ring
The bell that calls us on: the sweet far thing.
Beauty grown sad with its eternity
Made you of us, and of the dim gray sea.
Our long ships loose thought-woven sails and wait,
For God has bid them share an equal fate;
And when at last defeated in His wars,
They have gone down under the same white stars,
We shall no longer hear the little cry
Of our sad hearts, that may not live nor die.

W. B. YEATS
Poems (1899)

A LANE IN FEBRUARY

I wandered up this way last year;
    Unchanged, unmoved, it may not be
    Unlike what then it seemed to me;
The same dull ivied trees, and here
    The same black hedges that gird in
    Downs barren as the breasts of sin,
The same still wearied atmosphere.

And then as now I slowly passed
    Along the steep divided slope,
    With aching heart and without hope,
Scarce caring in what shape the last
    Blow fell upon my beaten brow,
    With eyes foreseeing then as now
The future blacker than the past.

What has the year left with me? One
    Sad love destroyed through time and scorn;
    A summer of delight forlorn;
Memories of sorrows that are gone
    With grey and desolated hours;
    And this dry handful of spoilt flowers
That died as I laid hand thereon.

THEODORE WRATISLAW
Love's Memorial (1892)

INTO THE TWILIGHT

Out-worn heart, in a time out-worn,
Come clear of the nets of wrong and right;
Laugh heart again in the gray twilight,
Sigh, heart, again in the dew of the morn.

Your mother Erie is always young,
Dew ever shining and twilight gray;
Though hope fall from you and love decay,
Burning in fires of a slanderous tongue.

Come, heart, where hill is heaped upon hill:
For there the mystical brotherhood
Of sun and moon and hollow and wood
And river and stream work out their will;

And God stands winding His lonely horn,
And time and the world are ever in flight;
And love is less kind than the gray twilight,
And hope is less dear than the dew of the morn.

W. B. YEATS
The Wind Among the Reeds (1899)

BY THE POOL AT THE THIRD ROSSES

I heard the sighing of the reeds
In the grey pool in the green land,
The sea-wind in the long reeds sighing
Between the green hill and the sand.

I heard the sighing of the reeds
Day after day, night after night;
I heard the whirring wild ducks flying,
I saw the sea-gull's wheeling flight.

I heard the sighing of the reeds
Night after night, day after day,
And I forgot old age, and dying,
And youth that loves, and love's decay.

I heard the sighing of the reeds
At noontide and at evening,
And some old dream I had forgotten
I seemed to be remembering.

I hear the sighing of the reeds:
Is it in vain, is it in vain
That some old peace I had forgotten
Is crying to come back again?

ARTHUR SYMONS
Images of Good and Evil (1899)

A LAST WORD

Let us go hence: the night is now at hand;
    The day is overworn, the birds all flown;
    And we have reaped the crops the gods have sown;
Despair and death; deep darkness o'er the land,
Broods like an owl; we cannot understand
    Laughter or tears, for we have only known
    Surpassing vanity: vain things alone
Have driven our perverse and aimless band.

Let us go hence, somewhither strange and cold,
  To Hollow Lands where just men and unjust
  Find end of labour, where's rest for the old,
Freedom to all from love and fear and lust.
Twine our torn hands! O pray the earth enfold
Our life-sick hearts and turn them into dust.

ERNEST DOWSON
Decorations (1899)

NIHILISM

Among immortal things not made with hands;
Among immortal things, dead hands have made:
Under the Heavens, upon the Earth, there stands
Man's life, my life: of life I am afraid.

Where silent things, and unimpassioned things,
Where things of nought, and things decaying, are:
I shall be calm soon, with the calm, death brings.
The skies are gray there, without any star.

Only the rest! the rest! Only the gloom,
Soft and long gloom! The pausing from all thought!
My life, I cannot taste: the eternal tomb
Brings me the peace, which life has never brought.

For all the things I do, and do not well;
All the forced drawings of a mortal breath:
Are as the hollow music of a bell,
That times the slow approach of perfect death.

LIONEL JOHNSON
Ireland, with Other Poems (1897)

A SHROPSHIRE LAD

54

With rue my heart is laden
    For golden friends I had,
For many a rose-lipt maiden
    And many a lightfoot lad.

By brooks too broad for leaping
    The lightfoot boys are laid;
The rose-lipt girls are sleeping
    In fields where roses fade.

A. E. HOUSMAN
A Shropshire Lad (1896)

THE GARDEN OF SHADOW

Love heeds no more the sighing of the wind
Against the perfect flowers: thy garden's close
Is grown a wilderness, where none shall find
One strayed, last petal of one last year's rose.

O bright, bright hair! O mouth like a ripe fruit!
Can famine be so nigh to harvesting?
Love, that was songful, with a broken lute
In grass of graveyards goeth murmuring.

Let the wind blow against the perfect flowers,
And all thy garden change and glow with spring:
Love is grown blind with no more count of hours,
Nor part in seed-time nor in harvesting.

ERNEST DOWSON
Verses (1896)

THE FALLING OF THE LEAVES

Autumn is over the long leaves that love us,
And over the mice in the barley sheaves;
Yellow the leaves of the rowan above us,
And yellow the wet wild-strawberry leaves.

The hour of the waning of love has beset us,
And weary and worn are our sad souls now;
Let us part, ere the season of passion forget us,
With a kiss and a tear on thy drooping brow.

W. B. YEATS
Poems (1899)

ENNUI

Alas! and oh that Spring should come again
Upon the soft wings of desired days,
And bring with her no anodyne to pain,
And no discernment of untroubled ways.
There was a time when her yet distant feet,
Guessed by some prescience more than half divine,
Gave to my listening ear such happy warning,
    That fresh, serene, and sweet,
My thoughts soared up like larks into the morning,
From the dew-sprinkled meadows crystalline.

Soared up into the heights celestial,
And saw the whole world like a ball of fire,
Fashioned to be a monster playing ball
For the enchantment of my young desire.

And yesterday they flew to this black cloud,
(Missing the way to those ethereal spheres.)
And saw the earth a vision of affright,
   And men a sordid crowd,
And felt the fears and drank the bitter tears,
And saw the empty houses of Delight.

The sun has sunk into a moonless sea,
And every road leads down from Heaven to Hell,
The pearls are numbered on youth's rosary,
I have outlived the days desirable.
What is there left? And how shall dead men sing
Unto the loosened strings of Love and Hate,
Or take strong hands to Beauty's ravishment?
   Who shall devise this thing,
To give high utterance to Miscontent,
Or make Indifference articulate?

LORD ALFRED DOUGLAS
The City of the Soul (1899)

MICHAEL ROBARTES BIDS HIS
BELOVED BE AT PEACE

I hear the Shadowy Horses, their long manes a-shake,
Their hoofs heavy with tumult, their eyes glimmering white;
The North unfolds above them clinging, creeping night,
The East her hidden joy before the morning break,
The West weeps in pale dew and sighs passing away,
The South is pouring down roses of crimson fire:
O vanity of Sleep, Hope, Dream, endless Desire,
The Horses of Disaster plunge in the heavy clay:

Beloved, let your eyes half close, and your heart beat
Over my heart, and your hair fall over my breast,
Drowning love's lonely hour in deep twilight of rest,
And hiding their tossing manes and their tumultuous feet.

W. B. YEATS
The Wind Among the Reeds (1899)

MYSTIC AND CAVALIER

Go from me: I am one of those, who fall.
What! hath no cold wind swept your heart at all,
In my sad company? Before the end,
    Go from me, dear my friend!

Yours are the victories of light: your feet
Rest from good toil, where rest is brave and sweet.
But after warfare in a mourning gloom,
    I rest in clouds of doom.

Have you not read so, looking in these eyes?
Is it the common light of the pure skies,
Lights up their shadowy depths? The end is set:
    Though the end be not yet.

When gracious music stirs, and all is bright,
And beauty triumphs through a courtly night;
When I too joy, a man like other men:
    Yet, am I like them, then?

And in the battle, when the horsemen sweep
Against a thousand deaths, and fall on sleep:
Who ever sought that sudden calm, if I
    Sought not? Yet, could not die.

Seek with thine eyes to pierce this crystal sphere:
Canst read a fate there, prosperous and clear?
Only the mists, only the weeping clouds:
    Dimness, and airy shrouds.

Beneath, what angels are at work? What powers
Prepare the secret of the fatal hours?
See! the mists tremble, and the clouds are stirred:
    When comes the calling word?

The clouds are breaking from the crystal ball,
Breaking and clearing: and I look to fall.
When the cold winds and airs of portent sweep,
    My spirit may have sleep.

O rich and sounding voices of the air!
Interpreters and prophets of despair:
Priests of a fearful sacrament! I come,
    To make with you mine home.

LIONEL JOHNSON
Poems (1895)

DREGS

The fire is out, and spent the warmth thereof,
(This is the end of every song man sings!)
The golden wine is drunk, the dregs remain,
Bitter as wormwood and as salt as pain;
And health and hope have gone the way of love
Into the drear oblivion of lost things.
Ghosts go along with us until the end;
This was a mistress, this, perhaps, a friend.

With pale, indifferent eyes, we sit and wait
For the dropt curtain and the closing gate:
This is the end of all the songs man sings.

ERNEST DOWSON
Decorations (1899)

A SHROPSHIRE LAD

7

When smoke stood up from Ludlow,
    And mist blew off from Teme,
And blithe afield to ploughing
    Against the morning beam
    I strode beside my team,

The blackbird in the coppice
    Looked out to see me stride,
And hearkened as I whistled
    The trampling team beside,
    And fluted and replied:

'Lie down, lie down, young yeoman;
    What use to rise and rise?
Rise man a thousand mornings
    Yet down at last he lies,
    And then the man is wise.'

I heard the tune he sang me,
    And spied his yellow bill;
I picked a stone and aimed it,
    And threw it with a will:
    Then the bird was still.

Then my soul within me
   Took up the blackbird's strain,
And still beside the horses
   Along the dewy lane
   It sang the song again:

'Lie down, lie down, young yeoman;
   The sun moves always west;
The road one treads to labour
   Will lead one home to rest,
   And that will be the best.'

A. E. HOUSMAN
A Shropshire Lad (1896)

THE DARKLING THRUSH

I leant upon a coppice gate
   When Frost was spectre-gray,
And Winter's dregs made desolate
   The weakening eye of day.
The tangled bine-stems scored the sky
   Like strings from broken lyres,
And all mankind that haunted nigh
   Had sought their household fires.

The land's sharp features seemed to be
   The Century's corpse outleant,
His crypt the cloudy canopy,
   The wind his death-lament.
The ancient pulse of germ and birth
   Was shrunken hard and dry,
And every spirit upon earth
   Seemed fervourless as I.

At once a voice outburst among
    The bleak twigs overhead
In a full-hearted evensong
    Of joy illimited;
An aged thrush, frail, gaunt, and small,
    In blast-beruffled plume,
Had chosen thus to fling his soul
    Upon the growing gloom.

So little cause for carollings
    Of such ecstatic sound
Was written on terrestrial things
    Afar or nigh around,
That I could think there trembled through
    His happy good-night air
Some blessed Hope, whereof he knew
    And I was unaware.

December 1900

THOMAS HARDY
Poems of the Past and Present (1902)

ENVOY

Go, songs, for ended is our brief, sweet play;
    Go, children of swift joy and tardy sorrow:
And some are sung, and that was yesterday,
    And some unsung, and that may be to-morrow.

Go forth; and if it be o'er stony way,
    Old joy can lend what newer grief must borrow:
And it was sweet, and that was yesterday,
    And sweet is sweet, though purchasèd with sorrow.

Francis Thompson

Go, songs, and come not back from your far way:
  And if men ask you why ye smile and sorrow,
Tell them ye grieve, for your hearts know To-day,
  Tell them ye smile, for your eyes know To-morrow.

FRANCIS THOMPSON
New Poems (1897)

BIOGRAPHICAL AND
BIBLIOGRAPHICAL NOTES

In the following notes a short account of each poet's life is followed
by a brief bibliography listing under (a) his main books of poems,
and under (b) a very select list of books which may provide a starting
point for critical or biographical study.

ALFRED AUSTIN (1835–1913) was born in Leeds, graduated from
London University, and was called to the bar in 1857. He aban-
doned law for literature in 1858, and thereafter as poet, critic,
editor, and journalist, he won enough support to earn him the
laureateship in 1896, although critics have consistently, and by and
large justifiably, felt that his successes are few and mostly in prose.

(a) *Interludes* (1872); *Soliloquies in Song* (1882); *Love's Widowhood*
(1889); *Lyrical Poems* (1891); *Narrative Poems* (1891); *Songs of
England* (1891); *England's Darling* (1896); *The Conversion of
Winckelmann* (1897); *A Tale of True Love* (1902); *Victoria the
Wise* (1903); *Sacred and Profane Love* (1908).
(b) *The Autobiography of Alfred Austin, Poet Laureate, 1835–1910*
(1911); Norton B. Crowell, *Alfred Austin: Victorian* (1955).

JOHN EVELYN BARLAS (1860–1914) published under the
pseudonym 'Evelyn Douglas'. Born in Burma and educated at New
College, Oxford, he took posts as a teacher while pursuing in his
own time his twin enthusiasms, poetry and socialism. He took part
in some of the violent socialist demonstrations in the 'eighties and
it may have been a blow received at one of these that led the way to
his insanity. He spent most of his later years in an asylum.

(a) *Poems, Lyrical and Dramatic* (1884); *Bird-Notes* (Chelmsford,
1887); *Dream-Fugues* (Chelmsford, 1887); *Holy of Holies*
(1887); *Love Sonnets* (Chelmsford, 1889); *Selections from
'Songs of a Bayadere' and 'Songs of a Troubadour'* (Dundee,

1893); H. S. Salt, ed., *Selections from the Poems of John E. Barlas* (1925).

(b) David Lowe, *John Barlas, Sweet Singer and Socialist* (Cupar, 1915).

AUBREY BEARDSLEY (1872–98), primarily a draughtsman, rose rapidly to fame after his designs for *Morte d'Arthur* in 1893. Art editor for the first four volumes of *The Yellow Book* (1894–5) and for *The Savoy* (1896), and designer of covers and decorations for many books which caught the public eye, he had achieved an influential body of work before he died, a convert to Roman Catholicism, in Menton. The three poems here are virtually the sum of his achievement in verse.

(a) *Under the Hill, and Other Essays in Prose and Verse* (1904).

(b) Stanley Weintraub, *Beardsley* (1967); Brian Reade, *Beardsley* (1967); Brigid Brophy, *Black and White* (1968).

ROBERT LAURENCE BINYON (1869–1943), poet, art-historian, and critic, was born in Lancaster. Newdigate Prize winner with *Persephone* (Oxford, 1890), he became Keeper of prints and drawings in the British Museum, where he worked for forty years, becoming an authority on Oriental art, but never losing his interest in poetry.

(a) *Lyric Poems* (1894); *Poems* (Oxford, 1895); *The Praise of Life* (1896); *First Book of London Visions* (1896); *Porphyrion* (1898); *Second Book of London Visions* (1899); *Odes* (1901); *The Death of Adam* (1904); *England* (1909); *Auguries* (1913); *The Cause* (1917); *For the Fallen* (1917); *The New World* (1918); *The Secret* (1920); *Collected Poems* (1931); *The North Star* (1941).

OLIVE ELEANOR CUSTANCE (1874–1944) became Lady Alfred Douglas after a runaway marriage in 1902. Though they were separated after eleven years, they remained on good terms. They had one son.

(a) *Opals* (1897); *Rainbows* (1902); *The Blue Bird* (1905); *The Inn of Dreams* (1911).

JOHN DAVIDSON (1857–1909), the son of a minister of the

Evangelical Union, left the variety of jobs he had held in Scotland to make a living by his pen in London, where he wrote plays, novels, poems and criticism. A member of the Rhymers' Club, he was nonetheless hostile to the less vigorous elements of the age. Though he achieved some popularity with his *Fleet Street Eclogues*, he always found difficulty in supporting his family. His stance became increasingly Nietzschean and assertive. He drowned himself in 1909.

(a) *In a Music-Hall* (1891); *Fleet Street Eclogues* (1893); *Ballads and Songs* (1894); *A Second Series of Fleet Street Eclogues* (1896); *New Ballads* (1897); *The Last Ballad* (1899); *Testaments* (1901); *The Testament of a Prime Minister* (1904); *Holiday* (1906); *The Testament of John Davidson* (1908); *Fleet Street* (1909); Maurice Lindsay, ed., *John Davidson, a Selection of his Poems* (1961).

(b) James B. Townsend, *John Davidson, Poet of Armageddon* (New Haven, 1961).

RICHARD WATSON DIXON (1833–1900), son of a Methodist minister, was an Anglican minister in Northumberland and Cumberland. At Oxford he knew Burne-Jones, Morris, and Rossetti. His poetry and his writing on ecclesiastical history are not as well known as his friendship and correspondence with Gerard Manley Hopkins.

(a) *Christ's Company* (1861); *Mano* (1883); *Odes and Eclogues* (Oxford, 1884); *Lyrical Poems* (Oxford, 1887); *Songs and Odes* (1896); *The Last Poems of Richard Watson Dixon* (1905); *Poems* (1909).

(b) Claude C. Abbott, ed., *The Correspondence of Gerard Manley Hopkins and Richard Watson Dixon* (Oxford, 1955); (Arthur) James Sambrook, *A Poet Hidden* (1962).

LORD ALFRED DOUGLAS (1870–1945), son of the 8th Marquis of Queensberry, educated at Winchester and Magdalen College, Oxford, is popularly known for his involvement with Oscar Wilde. He married Olive Custance in 1902. His name is usually associated with that of Wilde, but his verse is worthy of consideration in its own right, and his prickly autobiographical work is of interest.

(a) *Poèmes* (Paris, 1896); *The City of the Soul* (1899); *Complete Poems* (1928); *Lyrics* (1935); *Sonnets* (1935).

(b) *The Autobiography of Lord Alfred Douglas* (1929); Rupert C. Cooke, *Bosie* (1963).

ERNEST CHRISTOPHER DOWSON (1867–1900), son of the owner of a dry-dock, had an irregular education, frequently on the Continent. He gave up his course at Queen's College, Oxford, and for a time mixed work in his father's declining business with associating with other writers, notably at the Rhymers' Club. He always moved freely between England and France, and was until his death from consumption always on good terms with his fellow poets and translators. His unreturned devotion to a young girl is an important but often exaggerated feature of his life.

(a) *Verses* (1896); *Decorations* (1899); Desmond Flower, ed., *The Poetical Works of Ernest Dowson* (3rd edition, 1967).

(b) Thomas B. Swann, *Ernest Dowson* (New York, 1964); Desmond Flower and Henry Maas, eds., *The Letters of Ernest Dowson* (1967); Mark Longaker, *Ernest Dowson* (3rd edition, 1967).

MICHAEL FIELD was the pseudonym of two women, Katharine Harris Bradley (1846–1914) and her niece Edith Emma Cooper (1862–1913). Being of independent means, they devoted themselves to literature; but though their early dramatic work received encouragement even from Browning, their tragedies, of which they wrote over two dozen, have more fire than form and share with much Victorian poetic drama an unsuitability for the stage. A brief association with the newer trends of the 'nineties soon ended. They continued writing poems, plays, and their fascinating diaries, until their deaths, a year apart, of cancer.

(a) *Long Ago* (1889); *Sight and Song* (1892); *Underneath the Bough* (1893); *Wild Honey from Various Thyme* (1908); *Poems of Adoration* (1912); *Mystic Trees* (1913); *Dedicated* (1914); T. Sturge Moore, ed., *A Selection from the Poems* (1923); *The Wattlefold* (1930).

(b) Mary C. Sturgeon, *Michael Field* (1922); T. and D. C. Sturge Moore, eds., *Works and Days* (1933).

JOHN GRAY (1866–1934) held positions in the General Post Office and the Foreign Office for a while. He met Oscar Wilde, published the exquisite *Silverpoints* (1893), but abandoned the exaggerated pose of that volume not only to write predominantly religious poetry, but also to take orders; he had become a Roman Catholic in 1890. He lived and performed his duties mostly in Edinburgh, where he lived with his friend André Raffalovich.

(a) *Silverpoints* (1893); *Spiritual Poems* (1896); *Ad Matrem* (1904); *The Long Road* (1926); *Poems, 1931* (1931).

(b) Brocard Sewell, ed., *Two Friends: John Gray and André Raffalovich* (Aylesford, 1963); Brocard Sewell, *Footnote to the Nineties* (1968).

GEORGE ARTHUR GREENE (1853–1921) was born and educated in Florence, though he was of Anglo-Irish stock. After his first in modern literature at Trinity College, Dublin, he held a variety of lecturing and examining posts. He was one of several Irishmen in the Rhymers' Club, and was active in Irish matters, becoming Vice Chairman of the Irish Literary Society and working for the Irish Texts Society.

(a) *Italian Lyrists of To-day* (1893); *Dantesques* (1903); *Songs of the Open Air* (1912).

THOMAS HARDY (1840–1928) was born in Dorset. The son of a builder, he trained and for a short time practised as an architect. Although famous for his novels, which gave him sufficient income to abandon other work, Hardy had a lifelong love of poetry to which he increasingly devoted his attentions. He received the O.M. in 1910.

(a) *Wessex Poems* (1898); *Poems of the Past and Present* (1902); *Time's Laughingstocks* (1909); *Satires of Circumstance* (1914); *Moments of Vision* (1917); *Late Lyrics and Earlier* (1922); *Human Shows, Far Fantasies* (1925); *Winter Words* (1928); *Collected Poems* (4th edition, 1930).

(b) Florence E. Hardy, *The Early Life of Thomas Hardy, 1840–91* (1928) and *The Later Years of Thomas Hardy, 1892–1928* (1930).

A useful guide to further reading will be found in Irving Howe's *Thomas Hardy* (1968).

WILLIAM ERNEST HENLEY (1849-1903) was born in Gloucester, the son of a bookseller. He was a cripple from boyhood, losing one foot and in danger of losing the other until he came under Lister's care in Edinburgh Infirmary. A friend of Robert Louis Stevenson, with whom he collaborated on four plays, and editor of several papers, including the *Scots Observer*, later the *National Observer*, he balanced by his vigorous style and attitude his constrained and painful existence.

(a) *A Book of Verses* (1888); *The Song of the Sword* (1892; 2nd edition, called *London Voluntaries*, 1893); *Poems* (1898); *London Types* (1898); *Hawthorn and Lavender* (1899); *For England's Sake* (1900); *A Song of Speed* (1903); *The Works of W. E. Henley* (1908); *The Works of William Ernest Henley* (1921).

(b) Jerome H. Buckley, *William Ernest Henley* (Princeton, 1945).

HERBERT PERCY HORNE (1864–1916), art-historian, architect, typographer, designer, and poet, was involved in the foundation of the Century Guild and in the editing of its magazines, the *Century Guild Hobby Horse* and the *Hobby Horse*. A permanent guest at the Rhymers' Club, Horne later lived in Italy, where the Fondazione Horne still exists.

(a) *Diversi Colores* (1891).

ALFRED EDWARD HOUSMAN (1859–1936) was born in Worcestershire. Despite a disappointment in his results at Oxford, he returned to university life in 1892, after ten years in the Patent Office, to take the Chair of Latin at University College, London, from which he moved to a similar chair at Cambridge in 1911. A meticulous editor of Manilius and other writers, a witty and severe critic, he is best known for his small corpus of poems, the ideas behind which can be seen in *The Name and Nature of Poetry* (1933).

(a) *A Shropshire Lad* (1896); *Last Poems* (1922); *More Poems* (1936); John W. Carter, ed., *The Collected Poems of A. E. Housman* (1939).

Biographical and Bibliographical Notes

(b) Christopher Ricks, ed., *A. E. Housman*, Twentieth Century Views (Englewood Cliffs, N.J., 1968).

SELWYN IMAGE (1859–1930), scholar, artist, and poet, co-founded with Stewart Headlam the Church and Stage Guild, and helped in the production of the *Century Guild Hobby Horse*. The house at 20 Fitzroy Street which he occupied until 1917 was, in the 'nineties, a centre for artistic activity. He devoted himself religiously to art, and was Slade Professor of Fine Arts at Oxford from 1910 to 1916.

(a) *Poems and Carols* (1894); Arthur H. Mackmurdo, ed., *The Poems of Selwyn Image* (1932).

(b) Arthur H. Mackmurdo, ed., *Selwyn Image, Letters* (1932).

LIONEL PIGOT JOHNSON (1867–1902) was born at Broadstairs and educated at Winchester and New College, Oxford. He was a scholar and a traditionalist, influenced by Celticism, the Classics, and Catholicism, his adopted religion. His criticism, in the school of Arnold and Pater, is revealing and incisive, his poems are cold and clear. Yeats in *Autobiographies* and 'In Memory of Major Robert Gregory' remembers this fellow-member of the Rhymers' Club, and Pound refers to Johnson in 'Hugh Selwyn Mauberley'.

(a) *Poems* (1895); *Ireland, with Other Poems* (1897); Ezra Pound, ed., *Poetical Works* (1915); Iain Fletcher, ed., *The Complete Poems of Lionel Johnson* (1953).

(b) Arthur W. Patrick, *Lionel Johnson, poète et critique* (Paris, 1939).

RUDYARD KIPLING (1865–1936), born in Bombay but educated in England, returned to India in 1882 to become a journalist, but had achieved a name as a writer of verse and short stories by the time of his return to England in 1889. He was given the Nobel Prize for Literature in 1907, but his verse, with its patriotism and rather brass band style, has only recently returned to some critical praise.

(a) *Departmental Ditties* (1886); *Barrack-Room Ballads* (1892); *The Seven Seas* (1896); *Recessional, and Other Poems* (1899); *The*

Five Nations (1903); *Songs from Books* (1913); *The Years Between* (1918); *Rudyard Kipling's Verse. Definitive Edition* (1940).

(b) T. S. Eliot, *A Choice of Kipling's Verse* (1941); Charles Carrington, *Rudyard Kipling, his Life and Works* (1955); J. I. M. Stewart, *Eight Modern Writers* (1963).

EUGENE LEE-HAMILTON (1845–1907) spent his early life mainly on the Continent and was privately educated. Having won a scholarship to Oxford to study modern languages, he went down after two years without taking a degree. After six years in the Civil Service, he resigned in 1875 because of an illness which kept him bedridden for twenty years. The disease may well have been in part an escape from life, but he was cured and married in the 'nineties.

(a) *Poems and Transcripts* (1878); *Gods, Saints and Men* (1880); *The New Medusa* (1882); *Apollo and Marsyas* (1884); *Imaginary Sonnets* (1888); *Sonnets of the Wingless Hours* (1894); *Forest Notes* (with his wife, Annie E. Holdsworth, 1899).

RICHARD LE GALLIENNE (1866–1947) was born in Liverpool, where he trained for a short time as an accountant. He made his name in the 'nineties as poet, critic, and belle-lettrist; he was associated with the Rhymers' Club, and he was influential as reviewer and as reader for the firm of Mathews and Lane. He wrote too much and never regained the position he had in the 'nineties, a period with which he re-affirmed his connexion in his recollections of *The Romantic '90s* (1925).

(a) *My Ladies' Sonnets* (Liverpool, 1887); *English Poems* (1892); *Robert Louis Stevenson, an Elegy, and Other Poems* (1895); *Rubáiyát of Omar Khayyám: a Paraphrase* (1897); *New Poems* (1910); *The Lonely Dancer* (1914); *The Silk-Hat Soldier* (1915); *The Junk-Man* (1920); *A Jongleur Strayed* (1922).

(b) Geoffrey Smerdon and Richard Whittington-Egan, *The Quest of the Golden Boy* (1960).

ALICE CHRISTIANA MEYNELL (1847–1922), née Thompson married Wilfrid Meynell in 1877 and helped him to edit *Merry England*. A Catholic convert in the 'seventies, she was familiar with many Catholic writers, of the 'nineties like Francis Thompson or of an earlier period like Coventry Patmore, though she counted other writers like George Meredith among her friends. Her poems and numerous essays were written without noticeable effect from or on a family of eight children.

(a) *Preludes* (1875); *Poems* (1893); *Other Poems* (1896); *Later Poems* (1902); *The Shepherdess* (1914); *A Father of Women* (1917); *The Last Poems of Alice Meynell* (1923); *The Poems of Alice Meynell*, Oxford Standard Authors (1940).

(b) Viola Meynell, *Alice Meynell* (1929); Terence L. Connolly, ed., *Alice Meynell Centenary Tribute, 1847–1947* (Boston, 1948).

HENRY JOHN NEWBOLT (1862–1938), barrister, editor, author, and poet, was born at Bilston and educated at Clifton and Corpus Christi, Oxford. He practised law for some years, but continued to write, achieving an immediate popularity with his poems about the sea, which are still familiar both as recitation and song. He was knighted in 1915.

(a) *Admirals All* (1897); *The Island Race* (1898); *The Sailing of the Long Ships* (1902); *Clifton Chapel* (1908); *Songs of Memory and Hope* (1909); *Poems: New and Old* (1912); *St George's Day* (1918); *Collected Poems, 1897–1907* (1918); *A Perpetual Memory* (1939).

(b) *My World as in My Time* (1932); *The Later Life and Letters of Sir Henry Newbolt* (1942).

VINCENT O'SULLIVAN (1868–1940) was born in New York and educated there and at Exeter College, Oxford, where he did not graduate. His work was published by Leonard Smithers, and O'Sullivan was familiar with many of the authors he published. After the First World War he lectured at Rennes University, travelled, wrote, was injured in a street accident in 1932 and, though he had once been wealthy, died in poverty in Paris.

(a) *Poems* (1896); *The Houses of Sin* (1897).

(b) Alan Anderson, introd., *Opinions* (1959).

STEPHEN PHILLIPS (1864–1915) was educated at a variety of

places, and abandoned his studies for the Civil Service in order to join Sir Frank Benson's company. His stage experience made his poetic dramas more successful in the theatre than most of his Victorian predecessors, and he seemed to be entering the new century with great promise. It was not fulfilled, though he wrote several pieces. From 1913 to 1915 he edited the *Poetry Review*.

(a) *Orestes* (1884); in *Primavera* (1890); *Eremus* (1894); *Christ in Hades* (1896); *Poems* (1898); *New Poems* (1908); *The New Inferno* (1911); *Lyrics and Dramas* (1913); *Panama* (1915).

VICTOR GUSTAVE PLARR (1863–1929) was born near Strasbourg, his father Alsatian, his mother English. The family moved to England after the Franco-German war and Plarr studied modern history at Worcester College, Oxford. Though he continued his connexions with poets and poetry (he had been in the Rhymers' Club), he balanced that side of his work by his cataloguing and biographical works for the Royal College of Surgeons of England, whose librarian he was. Pound pictures him there as 'Monsieur Verog' in 'Hugh Selwyn Mauberley'.

(a) *In the Dorian Mood* (1896); *The Tragedy of Asgard* (1905).

(b) *Ernest Dowson, 1888–1897* (1914).

DOLLIE RADFORD (1858–1920), née Maitland, was born in Worcester and educated there, at Malvern, and at Queen's College, London. A member of the Fabian society, she had a life-long interest in Socialism, spending a good deal of time in the home of Karl Marx. She wrote for several magazines on artistic and literary topics. She married Ernest Radford in 1883.

(a) *A Light Load* (1891); *Songs for Somebody* (1893); *Good Night* (1895); *Songs and Other Verses* (1895); *A Ballad of Victory* (1907); *Poems* (1910).

ERNEST RADFORD (1857–1919) was born in Plymouth, went to Trinity Hall, Cambridge, and was called to the Bar in 1880. Though his poetry frequently reflects the legal background, he was known as an art critic and lecturer. He moved in Socialist and literary circles, was a member of the Rhymers' Club, and later knew Pound and Lawrence.

(a) *Translations from Heine* (1882); *Measured Steps* (1884); *Chambers Twain* (1890); *Old and New* (1895); *A Collection of Poems* (1906); *Songs in the Whirlwind* (with A. Radford, 1918).

ERNEST PERCIVAL RHYS (1859–1946) was born in Islington, and qualified and practised as a mining engineer before going to London in 1886 to begin a career whose most remarkable achievement is the editing of Everyman's Library. He was the only sign in the Rhymers' Club of a Welsh branch of the Celtic revival, and he recalls the period in his autobiographical work.

(a) *A London Rose* (1894); *Welsh Ballads* (1898); *The Leaf Burners* (1918); *Rhymes for Everyman* (1933); *Song of the Sun* (1937).
(b) *Everyman Remembers* (1931); *Letters from Limbo* (1936); *Wales England Wed* (1940).

ARTHUR WILLIAM SYMONS (1865–1945) educated himself by writing and lived by his pen. Having written a book (still of interest) on Browning when he was twenty-one, he rose rapidly to an influential position in the movements of the time, publishing poems, translations, essays, reviews, and editing among other things *The Savoy* (1896). A mental breakdown in 1908 substantially limited his abilities, but his influence as trendsetter and introducer of foreign ideas had already had its effect.

(a) *Days and Nights* (1889); *Silhouettes* (1892; 2nd edition, 1896); *London Nights* (1895; 2nd edition, 1897); *Amoris Victima* (1897); *Images of Good and Evil* (1899); *Poems* (1902); *The Fool of the World* (1906); *Knave of Hearts* (1913); *Love's Cruelty* (1923); *Collected Works* (1924, only nine volumes published); *Jezebel Mort* (1931).
(b) Roger Lhombreaud, *Arthur Symons* (1963).

FRANCIS THOMPSON (1859–1907) was born in Preston, the son of a physician. Intended first for the Roman Catholic priesthood and then for his father's profession, he failed to qualify for either. Having followed de Quincey's path into opium and squalor in London, he was befriended by the Meynells who provided both material and spiritual help. His irregular Muse failing after the early 'nineties, he wrote mainly reviews, which are of a high standard.

(a) *Poems* (1893); *Sister Songs* (1895); *New Poems* (1897); *The Works of Francis Thompson* (3 vols., 1913).

(b) P. Danchin, *Francis Thompson: la vie et l'oeuvre* (Paris, 1959); Peter Butter, *Francis Thompson* (1961); John Walsh, *Strange Harp, Strange Symphony* (1968).

THEODORE WILLIAM GRAF WRATISLAW (1871–1933) was born and educated at Rugby, became a solicitor, gave that up for a literary career in 1893, but found that, though he contributed to *The Yellow Book* and *The Savoy* and wrote two books of poems, his writing would not support him. He became a Civil Servant in 1895, working in the Estate Office at Somerset House, but he published only one new poem in the twentieth century.

(a) *Love's Memorial* (Rugby, 1892); *Some Verses* (Rugby, 1892); *Caprices* (1893); *Orchids* (1896).

(b) John Gawsworth, ed., *Selected Poems* (1935).

WILLIAM BUTLER YEATS (1865–1939) was born at Sandymount, near Dublin. His life, from his early experiences of Ireland and London, his art school training, his love for Maud Gonne, to his winning of the Nobel Prize, appointment to the Irish Senate, and death at Cap Martin, has been written by Joseph Hone and by A. N. Jeffares. Undisputably one of the great poets of the twentieth century, the significance of the 'nineties in his development is that it was a period of searching for a stance, a style, a mask, a period of forming his ideas, and of course a time when he was learning his trade.

(a) *The Wanderings of Oisin* (1889); *The Countess Kathleen, and Various Legends and Lyrics* (1892); *Poems* (1895; revised 1899); *The Secret Rose* (1897); *The Wind Among the Reeds* (1899); *In the Seven Woods* (1903); *The Green Helmet* (1910); *Responsibilities* (1914); *The Wild Swans at Coole* (1919); *Michael Robartes and the Dancer* (1921); *Later Poems* (1922); *The Tower* (1928); *The Winding Stair* (1933); *Last Poems* (1939).

(b) Peter Ure's *Yeats* (revised edition, 1965), Balachandra

Rajan's *W. B. Yeats* (1965) and Raymond Cowell's *W. B. Yeats* (1969) each provides an introduction to Yeats and Yeats criticism; John Unterecker, *A Reader's Guide to William Butler Yeats* (1959) would help a new reader of Yeats, whose first venture further into Yeats criticism might usefully be A. G. Stock's *W. B. Yeats. His Poetry and Thought* (1961). The latest book on Yeats is Harold Bloom's *Yeats* (1970).

GENERAL BOOKS

Osbert Burdett, *The Beardsley Period* (1925).

J. A. V. Chapple, *Documentary and Imaginative Literature 1880–1920* (1970).

Barbara Charlesworth, *Dark passages: the Decadent Consciousness in Victorian Literature* (Madison, 1965).

David Daiches, *Some Late Victorian Attitudes* (1969).

Richard Ellmann, ed., *Edwardians and Late Victorians* (New York, 1959).

B. Ifor Evans, *English Poetry in the Later Nineteenth Century* (revised edition 1966).

Graham Hough, *The Last Romantics* (1949).

Holbrook Jackson, *The Eighteen Nineties* (1913).

Frank Kermode, *The Romantic Image* (1957).

Katherine L. Mix, *A Study in Yellow* (1960).

Ruth Z. Temple, *The Critic's Alchemy* (1953).

W. B. Yeats, *Autobiographies* (1926).

The reader might also be interested in the following three anthologies: A. J. A. Symons's *An Anthology of 'Nineties Verse* (1928) Martin Secker's *The Eighteen Nineties* (1948), and Karl Beckson's *Aesthetes and Decadents of the 1890's* (New York, 1966).

INDEX OF POETS

INDEX OF TITLES

Index of Titles

Index of Titles

Index of Titles

Index of Titles

INDEX OF FIRST LINES

Index of First Lines

Index of First Lines